Measures of Excellence
for School Library Media Centers

MEASURES OF EXCELLENCE
FOR SCHOOL LIBRARY MEDIA CENTERS

Edited by
David V. Loertscher

Libraries Unlimited, Inc.
Englewood, Colorado
1988

LIBRARIES UNLIMITED, INC.
P.O. Box 3988
Englewood, CO 80155-3988

Library of Congress Cataloging-in-Publication Data

Measures of excellence for school library media centers / edited by
David V. Loertscher.
  vii, 148 p. 17x25 cm.
  Articles reprinted from Drexel library quarterly (Nov. 1986) in
book form.
  Includes index.
  Contents: Collection mapping : an evaluation strategy for
collection development / David V. Loertscher -- Collection mapping :
the research / May Lein Ho and David V. Loertscher -- Collection
mapping and collection development / William Murray et al. -- Effect
of certain reporting techniques on instructional involvement of
library media specialists / Retta Patrick -- Personality and
communications behaviors of model school library media specialists /
Barbara Herrin, Louis R. Pointon, and Sara Russell -- Measures of
audiovisual production activities with students / Grace Donoho --
Media utilization in the classroom / Melvin McKinney Bowie --
Periodicals on microfiche / Thomas H. Olsen -- Standard measures for
sixteen-millimeter film libraries that support public schools /
Marvin Davis.
  ISBN 0-87287-652-7
  1. School libraries--Evaluation. 2. Media programs (Education)-
-Evaluation. 3. Audio-visual library service--Evaluation.
I. Loertscher, David V., 1940-
Z675.S3M333   1988
027.8--dc19   87-29802
                                                       CIP

Contents

Preface

This volume is a reprint of *Drexel Library Quarterly* volume 21, number 2, which was to be the Spring 1985 issue but which did not appear in print until November 1986.

The purpose of this collection of original articles is to provide seven very different evaluation measures for school library media services. These measures include collection mapping, involvement of teachers with library media specialists, student involvement in audiovisual production, library media specialist personality, media utilization in the classroom, and measures for 16mm film libraries that serve school library media programs. The central idea of the articles is that there should be a rethinking of the ways library media programs should be evaluated; that there are many measures which could be developed which would more nearly judge the impact that a library media program is having on the educational program of a school.

The author extends his appreciation to Anne B. Tanner, the managing editor of *Drexel Library Quarterly*, for her encouragement to reprint this issue and to the authors of the original articles who gave their permission for publication.

Introduction

A Modern Parable

It was heralded as the single most important spin-off of the tril-
lion-dollar Star Wars research project. The aidem. "Aidem," a
word which could be used either in the singular or plural, like
"sheep," was the latest in instructional technology. It was billed
as the most spectacular, the most basic of all learning devices ever
to hit the world of education. Almost every journal was filled with
descriptive and theoretical articles concerning aidem.

For once, AASL and AECT were in the forefront of an educational
technology. They formed a joint committee to study aidem and
within six months had produced national standards for this innovation. Every school, the associations pronounced, shall have
47.6 aidem per student. They must be purchased in a spectral
array of colors in the ratio of 9:6:5 proceeding from red to yellow
to blue. Aidem sizes should be ordered by the formula $Z =
F/piM$. Warehousing aidem in the school will require 3.64 pro-
fessionally certified aidem technologists with a minimum of 1.03
clericals per technologist. The annual budget for aidem should be
$353 per 1.85 students or 20 percent of the per-pupil operating
cost, whichever is greatest. Facilities for using aidem must be
built in a dome arising from the exact center of the school campus
and allow for every student to interact with an aidem of choice via
a specially constructed headset for a minimum of 43.7 minutes per
week.

Research studies showed that 75 percent of the teachers, 90 percent of the administrators and 57 percent of the library media
specialists favored aidem and were creating implementation strategies. Diffusion of the technology on a nationwide scale was un-
paralleled in the history of educational technology.

Some rumors were quashed which suggested that if students experienced a green aidem simultaneously with a blue aidem, a
slightly sensuous experience resulted. The underground press reported that red aidem were being used as substitute frisbees and

that yellow aidem used during physical exercise produced psychological highs if the pulse rate was above 117.

The Secretary of Education called a national conference to consider aidem. The most prestigious educators, researchers, government bureaucrats, school administrators and a few school board members were invited. Calls for papers produced a blizzard of presentations concerning the installation of aidem in the schools, costs, facilities, acquisition problems and color balance. The capstone was a distinguished panel with the Secretary of Education as moderator. After the panelists' responses, the Secretary called for questions from the audience. A school board member from Centerton, Iowa, was first at the microphones. "I would like to ask the distinguished panel," he said, "exactly what are the benefits of aidem to assist students in learning?" A hush spread over the hall; the panel bowed their heads; the Secretary's face turned red. Happily, a fire drill siren wailed and the conference closed prematurely. The press reported the success of the event and everyone went back home to buy more and more aidem than ever.

Evaluation of School Libraries

During the early part of the twentieth century, school libraries, like "aidem," were coming into existence in the nation's schools. Unlike aidem, excitement was never great and so progress was slow. In fact, it has been seventy years since school libraries began to develop in any measurable way, yet there are still some schools without them.

National professional associations, accrediting associations, and state departments of education have issued standards documents for school libraries over the past seventy years and, like the aidem standards, these documents have provided guidelines for numbers of items, staff size, facilities, and size of budget. These guidelines have been specific and measurable. For example, the 1925 standards for school libraries emphasize such things as "one-third of the total number of chairs should be 14" high, and two-thirds should be 18" high—the 14" chairs to match the 24" tables and the 18" chairs to match the 28" tables."[1] Such details take up numerous pages of the document.

Introduction

Modern standards are not quite as specific as their predecessors.
The 1975 standards state that every school should have "8,000 to
12,000 volumes or 16 to 24 per user."[2] Accrediting documents
contain similar lists of items, facilities, budgets, and staff which
each school should have if minimal accreditation is merited.

All of these documents contain descriptive statements of the "program" of the school library media center and provide guidance on
the types of services and the educational benefits to be expected
from the center. However, none of the services listed in the standards is stated in measurable terms. The lack of measurable
statements is not due to a lack of interest, but to a lack of ways to
measure such things as the amount of enjoyment derived from
reading a book or seeing a filmstrip.

Evaluative documents, which have been created for school libraries since the 1920s, have stressed the same things that standards have stressed: things, people, space, and money. While
these instruments are valuable as library media centers come into
existence and are of peripheral interest as library media centers
age, new evaluative instruments are needed to push on beyond
this beginning stage.

Everyone would like an evaluative thermometer which could test
the temperature of the library media program. Does a bubbly and
creative program increase test scores? That is the central question
for an educational community eagerly trying to justify its existence to the general public. Recently, Melvin Bowie[3] and Elaine
Didier[4] have done extensive reviews of the research in this area
and are fairly positive about the contribution of the library media
program to learning, yet neither can cite a simple thermometer test
of value. The problems of creating such a test are shared by the
rest of education and the social sciences as well. Solid, quantifi-
able evidence is difficult to collect.

Evaluative Documents

There have been a number of evaluative documents for school library media programs developed over the past ten years which
have departed from a quantitative count of things. These documents have generally measured services and have been valuable
in gauging perceptions and in planning efforts. The instruments of

Introduction

Liesener,[5] and Loertscher and Stroud[6] have been circulated widely and have been used to begin searching for impact of library media services. Zweizig, Braune and Waity[7] have recently issued evaluative measures for children's services in public libraries. Their measures concentrate on the numbers of patrons served and items circulated. The one measure they propose which would be applicable for school libraries is the reference fill rate—a measure of success and failure.

The current collection of articles for *Drexel Library Quarterly* represents a second step in the creation of evaluative documents for school library media programs. Within the articles of the issue are measures that suggest some newer directions. Space limitations allow for only a few of these newer measures, but they hint at future directions. Some analysis of these measures is in order.

The articles by Loertscher, Murray et al., and Ho & Loertscher look at collection mapping as a technique of collection development and evaluation. The Loertscher article presents the theory of collection mapping, the Ho and Loertscher article presents the supporting research, and the Murray et al. article presents collection mapping as applied in the Aurora, Colorado, schools. Together, these authors propose a system of making the collection accountable to the curriculum of a school and creating a collection map which will communicate collection strengths and weaknesses to a person who has never had any training in library science or instructional technology. This evaluative measure can help administrators track the dollars spent on collections in terms of the benefits to instructional units taught in the school. Both collection quality and quantities are assessed.

The article by Retta Patrick provides a measure to track involvement by library media specialists in instructional planning. The technique presented is essentially a tally sheet which records the occurrence of a particular action or service. The technique is not new, but its method of application is. Here, a top priority service, assumed to have a direct impact on instruction, is measured. The interesting finding is that when library media specialists are expected to behave in a certain way and know that their services are being measured, their behavior changes. In this study, the amount of instructional planning doubled in one year. The significance of the measure lies in its use. There is a clear role expec-

Introduction

tation as a prelude to action (we expect you to be involved in instructional development), a clear measurement of the role is taken, and a reward system is installed. The results are not surprising.

The article by Barbara Herrin provides a peek into the personality of the successful school library media specialist. This "communication animal" can be profiled and common characteristics noted so that individuals can be counseled into the field. Practicing specialists can find areas for personal development that might be pursued. There is a great deal to be said in matching the right person to the right job. In addition, Herron's data show that school library media specialists have different personal characteristics from librarians in general.

Grace Donoho has a unique library media program which focuses its services toward the creation of audiovisual media by students. She uses the survey technique to measure the impact of her program on students. First, she measures how many students are familiar with the techniques for creating a wide variety of media—the results are impressive. Second, she asks her teachers to gauge the impact that AV production has on student motivation and on the use of print media. It does not take a PhD. to recognize impact here.

Melvin Bowie proposes a technique to probe the effective use by teachers of audiovisual media. Her technique is a simple success/failure measure. As such, it not only provides a measure of success but analyzes the reasons for failure. In addition, follow-up interviews ascertain the satisfaction of users and the long-term success of a procedure. The success/failure measure presented here is one example of many that could be created—each looking at a specific aspect of service.

The article by Tom Olsen is a direct output measure of a library service. The concern here is the success rate at which students find articles in periodicals which they locate in periodical indexes. By duplicating back issues on microfiche, library media specialists can increase student success rates by a full 10 percent. Such a measure, with its follow-up interviews, makes some assumptions about the information society. Finding references to topical articles of interest is only one step. Being accountable to provide the articles is a challenge to library media specialists. This article suggests that a major standard for a library media pro-

Introduction

gram should be a high success rate for finding appropriate materials.

Finally, Marvin Davis provides quantitative measures for regional film libraries, which have not been published before. His measures look at warehouse mechanisms which must be in place if films are to be provided to teachers when and where they need them. As a first step, it is quantitative; the second step, impact on learners, is yet to be created.

The Future of Evaluation

This issue provides a variety of new measures for school library media programs and merely suggests future directions. Perhaps a chart of the measures included will illustrate the trend:

Author(s)	Measure	What is measured
Loertscher, Ho and Murray et al.	Collection mapping	Collection strengths Collection response to curricular demands
Patrick	Time analysis	Involvement in instructional development
Herrin	Personality measures	The type of person who is a successful library media specialist
Donoho	Questionnaires	Familiarity with AV production techniques; impact of AV production on student motivation and interaction with print media
Bowie	Questionnaires	Proper utilization of AV media
Olsen	Tally sheets	Success rates of supplying articles to students who use periodical indexes
Davis	Output measures	Provision of film to classroom teachers from regional film libraries

Introduction

A first analysis of the measures shows that common evaluative techniques from the social sciences can be applied meaningfully to library media programs. These measures can be directed toward topics of interest to school administrators and to library media specialists who are interested in accountability. Only the Donoho article probes effects of the library media program on learning, but other measures provide direct antecedents to the learning environment; i.e., the right people must be available, collections must respond appropriately, library media specialists must be involved in instruction and learning activities, and teachers must use media properly.

The measures created for this issue will be extended in book-length treatises being written by the author,[8] who hopes these efforts will stimulate library media specialists to create and use measures which demonstrate excellence. Like the school board member from Centerton, Iowa, we must be concerned with the bottom line of library media programs: learning.

David V. Loertscher

Postscript

The editor wishes to express sincere appreciation to Carolyn Leonard, a graduate assistant in the Instruction Resources Education Program at the University of Arkansas for the many hours of reading and correcting the manuscript, suggesting major improvements, tracking citations, and printing out the manuscript. The issue would not have been completed without her competent help.

Notes

1 A Joint Committee of the National Education Association and the American Library Association, C. C. Certain, Chairman, *Elementary School Library Standards* (Chicago: American Library Association, 1925), p. 7.

2 American Association of School Librarians and Association for Educational Communications and Technology, *Media Programs: District and School* (Chicago: American Library Association, 1975), p. 70.

3 Melvin McKinney Bowie, "Do Media Programs Have an Impact on Achievement?" *Instructional Innovator* 29 (February 1984), pp. 18–20.

Introduction

4 Elaine K. Didier, "Research on the Impact of School Library Media Programs on Student Achievement—Implications for School Media Professionals," in: *School Library Media Annual 1984,* vol. 2 (Littleton, CO: Libraries Unlimited, 1984), pp. 343–61.

5 James W. Liesener, *A Systematic Process for Planning Media Programs* (Chicago: American Library Association, 1976).

6 David V. Loertscher, and Janet G. Stroud, *PSES: Purdue Self-Evaluation System for School Media Centers* (Fayetteville, AK: Hi Willow, 1976).

7 Douglas Zweizig, Joan A. Braune and Gloria A. Waity, *Output Measures for Children's Services in Wisconsin Public Libraries: A Pilot Project—1984–85* (Madison, WI: Wisconsin Division for Library Services, 1985).

8 David V. Loertscher, *Excellence in School Library Media Programs* (Fayetteville, AK: Hi Willow Research & Publishing, 1986).

Collection Mapping: An Evaluation Strategy for Collection Development

David V. Loertscher

What is the function of a library media collection in a school? There seem to be two answers to that question—an intellectual answer and an answer as practiced in the schools. The intellectual answer is so well known that it is a platitude: "The function of a library media collection is to serve the curriculum of a school." *Media Programs: District and School* provides a more lofty statement:

> The collection in each school is rich in breadth and depth of content and represents varied types of materials, points of view, and forms of expression. It provides a broad range of media formats and meets the requirements of all curriculum areas, accommodating diverse learning skills and styles of users at varying maturity and ability levels.[1]

As fine sounding as this goal is, school library media specialists generally do not carry out its direction. The collections they do build are influenced heavily by traditional practices and acquisition procedures. Cecil and Heaps, who wrote one of the earliest histories of school libraries,[2] describe the visit of a number of famous Americans to Europe in the early 1900s. They studied educational practice and brought back ideas which influenced American education. According to Cecil and Heaps, "These educational leaders and others of the day realized that the development of intelligent citizens depended not only upon teaching reading but also on providing reading opportunities. It was for the purpose of providing such opportunities that the school district libraries came into being."[3]

The main point made by Cecil and Heaps was that early school library collections were built as supplementary reading repositories. One doesn't have to be very old to remember regular visits to the school library to get a good book to read, and a helpful librarian who tried to find "the right book for the right reader at the right time." But collections designed to support supplementary reading and collections that support curriculum are two different collections!

Supplementary reading collections overlap public library collections and are common in schools today because the techniques of building school library collections have been taught in graduate library schools by public library-oriented professors. A common scenario in a public school today would reveal a school librarian surveying the community (the school setting, students, and general curriculum), selecting titles from current review periodicals, using recommended national lists such as *Children's Catalog,* creating a consideration file, and selecting considered titles in priority order at acquisition time. Such a practice is based on the philosophy that the school library collection should contain the best of what is published in a current year. This practice guarantees that a school will have a public library collection housed in a school. Library media specialists who have such collections find themselves constantly trying to impose a collection of materials on unwilling teachers and buying materials they "hope" will be useful to students and teachers. They have large blocks of materials on topics not covered in any of the curricular guides or textbooks and so must campaign to get the subject taught by a teacher lest the investment in the collection is a total waste. In addition, library media specialists tend to build collections matching their own interests, tastes, and subject knowledge from their college majors.

If a collection in a school library is to support the curriculum taught in the school, a selection procedure quite different from that pictured above must take place. Such a procedure is not well described in the literature but is practiced by a number of school library media specialists who have rejected many of the theoretical collection building practices and have opted for a more practical approach.

The Study of the School Curriculum

The foundation of a sound collection building policy for a school is formulated by doing an in-depth curricular study. This study might include:

1 A survey of mandated curriculum for the school and curriculum guides which are actually in use

2 A survey of textbook adoption cycles and textbook approaches to curriculum

3 A study of the faculty teaching style as it relates to the written curriculum

4 A survey of the curriculum developers of a school to identify their ideas and expectations

A full-scale study of the curriculum in a school and district will take time and effort. It is not usually a part of graduate library school curriculum and it is rarely a part of a school library media specialist's job description. One of the best ways to get acquainted with the curriculum is to attend curriculum committee and textbook selection committee meetings. Such attendance will provide advance warning of curricular change and a solid perspective of what "ought to be happening," in addition to the daily perspective of what is actually being taught.

If a library media specialist has this solid curriculum foundation, then a sound collection development policy and its accompanying method of implementation can be constructed. The purpose of this article is to suggest a new collection-building and evaluation strategy.

The Elephant Method of Collection Building

The sage advice that in order to eat an elephant, cut it into small pieces is a sound strategy for collection building. The idea is to divide a collection into a number of small but manageable segments which match the various parts of the curriculum. Each of these segments can be built, weeded, or maintained as curriculum needs dictate. Each segment has a corresponding piece of the total budget, depending on the priorities assigned to the goals of expansion, replacement only, or de-emphasis. These are the guidelines for school library media specialists: Do not build the collection as a whole. Build pieces of the collection. Create a collection that is tailored specifically for the school it serves.

For the purpose of collection development, the total collection should be divided into three major segments:

1 A basic collection designed to serve a wide variety of interests and needs. This collection provides breadth.

(2) General emphasis collections, which contain materials that support a whole course of instruction such as United States history or beginning reading. These collections provide intermediate depth in a collection.

(3) Specific emphasis collections, which contain materials that support units of instruction such as "Civil War" or "dinosaurs." These collections provide full depth and support as advocated by the national standards.

The mechanism by which a collection is divided into the three main collection segments, evaluated and then managed has been titled collection mapping.

Collection Mapping

A collection map is a visual supplement to the card catalog which graphically displays the breadth and depth of a library media collection. Such a map may be displayed as a large poster in the library media center where its function is to communicate collection strengths and needs to patrons. Each school's library media collection map might be completely different from the collection map of a neighboring school. Schools within a district or a region might have coordinated selection policies creating complementary collections which could be shared regularly. A sample collection is shown in table 1. This mapping technique was refined over a three-year period in two developmental studies. The first included over thirty schools whose library media specialists were in the author's classes, and the second was a formal national study conducted by Dr. May Lein Ho with the author's assistance at the University of Arkansas. Scales for the map were created from data in the national study. Charting an individual collection using the scales as shown above compares a school's collection with the national sample.

The selection of emphasis areas is the prerogative of the library media specialist and is based upon the curriculum of the school and the number of items which have been purchased in a topical area. Special collections, such as reference and periodicals, can be charted, and emphasis areas can be multimedia or a single medium. A collection map need not be static; that is, it can be recharted regularly as curricular shifts and collection shifts occur. It is evaluative in three aspects:

Collection Mapping: An Evaluation Strategy for Collection Development

Table 1
Collection Map

School name:
Number of students: 556
Total collection: 9,818
Number of total collection items per student: 17.65

	Number of items	Number of items per student
General Emphasis Areas:		
1. Biology	588	1.0575
2. Travel	376	.6762
3. Government	352	.6331
4. US history	234	.4208
Specific Emphasis Areas:		
5. Handicrafts	41	.0737
6. Space travel	60	.1079
7. Black history	81	.1456
Total:	1,732	

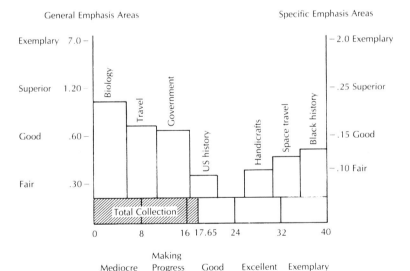

Note: Three component parts of a collection are charted. At the base of the map, the total collection is graphed horizontally and compared with the national standard of 40 items per student. This collection contains the basic collection and provides breadth. The general and specific emphasis areas are charted vertically on top of the total collection, each with its own scale of items per student.

Collection Mapping: An Evaluation Strategy for Collection Development

①Mapping will show collection strengths which can be compared to the curriculum of a school.

② Mapping will compare collection size in topical areas to a national sample of emphasis collections.

③ Mapping will show the quality of the collection as it responds to curricular demands.

A number of other uses of a collection map will be enumerated later in this article.

Creating a Collection Map

Creating a collection map is quite simple and takes three to five hours depending on the types of records kept and the experience which the person has with the collection. The technique is as follows:

1 Decide which general emphasis collections support whole courses of instruction, such as United States history, geography, art, etc. Count the number of items in the collection treating that topic (count the number of items available in each Dewey Decimal Class: Reference, 000, 100, 200 . . .).

2 Decide which specific emphasis collections support units of instruction, such as Civil War, insects, dinosaurs, etc. Count the number of items in the collection, treating each topic by Dewey Decimal class.

3 Divide the total size of each emphasis collection by the number of students in the school and chart the resulting items/student figure on the collection map.

4 If an emphasis collection is not large enough to be visible on the collection map, it should not be charted unless it is to become a target for collection development.

5 Divide the total size of the collection by the number of students in the school, and chart the result on the collection map under "total collection."

The worksheet in table 2 contains the data used to map the collection charted earlier in this article.

The collection map drawn from the information in the worksheet is a quantitative picture of a school library media collection. An

Collection Mapping: An Evaluation Strategy for Collection Development

Table 2
Collection Map Worksheet

School name:
Number of students: 556
Total number of items in the collection: 9,818
Number of total collection items per student: 17.65

Collection Segments

	Total	General Emphasis				Specific Emphasis		
		Biology	Travel	Government	US history	Black history	Handicrafts	Space travel
Reference	354	9	12	16	24	9	2	4
000	84							
100	86							
200	88							
300	1,194			306		32		
398.2 (elementary)								
400	164							
500	1,090	579						
600	942							32
700	620						39	
800	508							
900	1,522		345		145			
Biography	774		18	27		16		6
Fiction	2,182				63	24		16
Story Collection	98							
Easy (elementary)								
Periodicals	56		1	3	2			2
Professional Col.	56							
Total Segment	9,818	588	376	352	234	81	41	60
Items/Student	17.65	1.05	.67	.63	.42	.15	.07	.11

additional step must be taken to transform the map into a qualitative picture as well. This second step may take months to complete after the initial map is created and displayed to the general public.

Each of the segments of a collection map should be evaluated on how well it responds to the demands made upon it. A library media specialist might have been careful to choose "quality" materials in the first place, but those materials must stand the test of usefulness. Every time a major demand is placed upon one of the emphasis areas of the collection or upon the base (which is charted in the total collection), the library media specialist and the

Collection Mapping: An Evaluation Strategy for Collection Development

teacher should evaluate how well the collection responded. With input from the students, these two individuals can quickly rate the collection on the following criteria:

- Diversity of formats available (both books and AV)

- Recency of the collection (were the materials up-to-date?)

- Relevance of the collection to unit needs

- Duplication (were there enough materials for the number of students taught?)

- Reading/viewing/listening levels (were they appropriate for all students?)

If a rating scale is used with each of the above criteria (5 being high and 1 being low) and the average rating computed, then a quality score for that collection segment results. If the average rating is above 4.5, then a gold medal sticker should be affixed to the topic graphed on the collection map. If the average rating is above 4.0, a silver medal is given. A score above 3.0 gets a bronze sticker and scores below 3.0 get a frowning face sticker.

The resulting poster size map complete with graphs and stickers is an evaluative picture of the quantity and the quality of a library media collection.

Uses of the Collection Map

Thus far, a library media specialist who had been following the collection mapping technique, would have studied the curriculum of the school in depth and then created a poster-size collection map for public display. The next step is to make use of the map as a planning tool, a bragging tool, and a begging tool. Here are a few suggestions to make the tool effective.

1 A publicly displayed collection map draws the attention of faculty, students, administrators and parents to the strengths (and weaknesses) of a collection.

2 A collection map suggests the most logical areas of the curriculum that can be served most effectively. Conversely, curricular areas not charted show collection weaknesses.

3 A collection map might show purchasing targets and graph where the collection should be in a year (three years, five years, etc.).

4 Emphasis areas charted on the map which are not a part of the curriculum show segments which are irrelevant—topics that may have been supported in the past, but are taught no longer.

5 The collection map serves as a collection development tool. Library media specialists, teachers, and administrators can jointly decide what will happen to each of the emphasis segments. Will that part of the collection be strengthened? Will that topical area be maintained? Will that segment be allowed to die?

6 Consideration files for purchase will be divided into sections which match the segments charted on the collection map.

7 The collection map and the collection targets that result from it will have individual budget amounts assigned.

A Sample Collection Development Plan

Perhaps the best way to envision the use of a collection map is to examine how it would play a role in a total collection development plan. The following description of collection development procedure assumes that a library media specialist has automated most of the routine functions of the library media center. While a computer is not needed for the plan to work, the assumption is made that manual systems are being outdated rapidly.

Preliminary collection mapping: With or without a computer system, the library media specialist maps the collection. Meetings are held with the principal and teachers to discuss collection strengths and weaknesses and to create preliminary collection targets.

Computer system: The library media center has an integrated on-line catalog including four terminals (two for public access, one for circulation, and one for administrative use) connected to a 60 megabyte hard disk. Acquisition, cataloging, circulation, overdues, online catalog, and access to a network are components of the system.

Software:[4] A generic database and a word processor are part of the software package supplied by the vendor. One word processor file contains a master set of curricular units. Each record is something like a pathfinder containing unit title, teacher, dates taught, unit subject headings to probe in the catalog, outside resources called upon, and evaluative data concerning the role of the library media collection and services for that unit.

Collection Mapping: An Evaluation Strategy
for Collection Development

Acquisition system: A consideration file is kept on a computerized database. In addition to the usual information (author, title, etc.), entries are made for the teacher or department who requested the item, the name of the proposed unit(s) for which the item could be useful, and a priority rating. When an order is prepared, the library media specialists re-reads the goals and objectives of collection development and how much money has been targeted to collection segments, and then begins the selection process. The file is sorted by curricular unit and called up for examination. Priorities are examined and changed and items are selected until the planned budget is spent. Items for the base collection are selected on the basis of requests from students and teachers and an analysis of the reviews which have been published during the year. All items that are in the final selection are transmitted via modem to the vendor.

Cataloging system: When materials are received, they are sorted by curricular area with the aid of the acquisition database. Cataloging data are retrieved from a network. Call numbers and subject headings are adjusted as needed. One or several curricular unit codes or titles are added, like subject headings, so that a total bibliography can be printed as needed. The cataloging data is then added to the online catalog. As curricular changes occur, global changes in unit headings are made easily.

Unit planning: The library media specialists meets with a teacher for unit planning. The specialist comes to the meeting with a list of the resources, which has been printed out from the online catalog, and the unit "pathfinder" printed out from the word processor. The teacher and the specialist review the objectives of the unit, the pathfinder, and the bibliography and make their plans accordingly. Materials not available in the school are ordered from other schools, public libraries, regional collections, etc. Changes in the pathfinder and the bibliography are made on the computer as plans are finalized.

Unit evaluation: After the unit has been taught, the library media specialist and the teacher meet briefly to evaluate their success. The materials used are evaluated. If an emphasis area of the collection has been used, then an evaluative sticker is affixed to the collection map. The library media specialist adds materials that need replacing to the computer acquisition file and records the needs for additional purchase.

Collection map updating: Collection mapping is done annually, using the computerized unit bibliographies for emphasis area size figures. Collections developed or improved during the year are charted. Progress toward collection goals is summarized for annual reports. The poster-size collection map is updated for public display. Perhaps the old and new maps are displayed to show progress.

The Elephant Method in Perspective

Library media specialists who adopt the elephant method of collection development and use the collection mapping technique place themselves in a position to manage a collection and a collection development program. These persons see and understand curriculum structure and mesh a body of materials into that structure. The power to manage the whole comes from the management of simpler and smaller collection segments. Purchasing is done as a part of a systematic plan. The collection is accountable to curricular needs. Progress in collection building is apparent and more defensible. A dollar invested can be tracked in terms of outcome and use. Annual reports document impact on the curriculum—not aggregate collection size and circulation figures.

One of the greatest challenges of the collection manager is to plan amid change. Textbook cycles last five to seven years in many states and require adjustment of collections and even massive collection renewal at times. A bigger problem is change in teaching methodology and teaching styles as a result of teacher turnover. A science teacher in a building may use a variety of insect identification resources, another, biographical sources, and a third, none of these. Teachers who have been faithful users of library media collections might move to a new school. The temptation is often to ship a favorite body of materials with that teacher since no one else will likely use those materials. The changing picture here is a challenge to the collection manager. How nice it would be to resort to old collection building habits where the best of new publications are added each year and collection size and condition are the paramount concerns. The old method assumes that teachers must adapt to the library—not the library to the teacher. It assumes that teaching materials and library materials are two different things. It also guarantees that when budgets are tight, the library budget is a number-one target for reconsideration.

The elephant method structures the collection into segments understandable to non-library media specialists. In just a few moments, collection strengths and weaknesses can be perceived. Administrators and teachers who understand the composition of the collection can help determine which segments of the collection should be built, maintained or de-emphasized. Curricular change and its impact on library media collections can be understood and that impact measured. Sound long-range plans are possible based on curricular plans. One of the most important facets of the elephant method and the collection map is that the principal, who is the instructional leader of the school, can guide the direction of the curriculum with its accompanying teaching resources, can measure the impact of the library media collection, and can budget accordingly.

Variations on a Theme

Library media specialists are famous for taking an idea and improving upon it for a local situation and condition. The technique of collection development proposed here can be readily altered as needed, but as an evaluative tool it should not depart from the following guidelines:

1 A collection of materials should be broken down by curricular topics into segments small enough to manage easily.

2 Collection maps or other graphical or printed representations of collection strengths and weaknesses must be understandable to someone who has never had a course in library science or instructional technology.

3 The technique of collection segmentation should have a qualitative evaluation component—not just a quantitative one.

4 Any collection building technique must promote a systematic meshing of curricular targets and supporting teaching and learning materials. It must address both subject specialization needs and interdisciplinary possibilities.

5 The system must be simple.

For too long, collection building, collection sizes, and budgets in dollars per student have been mysterious ideas not well understood by administrators who were expected to be advocates for library media centers. Library media specialists must demonstrate to their publics that the money they spend can be tracked and that it fills specific needs in the curriculum. Arguments justifying library media collections must be as forceful as arguments supporting school bus fleets. Both require regular attention and renewal programs lest the health and well being of students be jeopardized. School buses, elephants, and collection maps may be factors worth library media specialists' attention.

Notes

1 American Association of School Librarians and Association For Educational Communications and Technology, *Media Programs: District and School* (Chicago: American Library Association, 1975), p. 68.

2 Henry L. Cecil and Willard A. Heaps, *School Library Service in the United States: An Interpretative Survey* (New York: H. W. Wilson, 1940).

3 Ibid., p. 41.

4 Most of the computer applications envisioned here can be performed with a single computer and good database and word processor programs. Examples would be Appleworks, PFS Write—File and Report, Dbase II, Applewriter, and many others.

Collection Mapping: The Research

May Lein Ho and David V. Loertscher

The mapping of a school library media collection is based on the philosophy that a collection in a school should serve the curriculum. Since the Dewey Decimal System does not organize a collection of materials to match the modern curriculum of a school, the technique of collection mapping was designed to serve as a bridge between curricular structure and materials organizational structure. In addition, collection mapping was designed to help build collection segments rather than selecting materials to add to an aggregate. The purpose of this study was to field test collection mapping as a technique and to amass enough data so that an individual school could compare its own collection against a national pool of school collections.

As the research was designed, two central questions emerged. What are the characteristics of school library media collections today when they are mapped? How do the collections in schools compare to nationally recommended lists such as *Elementary School Library Collection*,[1] *Junior High Library School Catalog*,[2] and *Senior High School Library Catalog*.[3] The following research report is divided into two segments for answering those two basic questions. Section one deals with collection mapping and section two compares school collections to nationally published basic materials lists.

Collection Mapping Research

The central question of exploring the characteristics of school library media collections using collection mapping was divided into several important sub-questions. What types of collections do school library media specialists build? Can the collection mapping technique be applied to a large number of schools in various geographical locations? Do charting techniques hold up under close scrutiny? Can a national data pool be developed which will allow school library media specialists to compare their collections with a national sample?

Collection Mapping: The Research

To explore these questions, questionnaires were sent to 120 library media specialists in elementary, junior high, and high schools in 11 states (Arkansas, Florida, Colorado, Connecticut, California, Iowa, Indiana, Oklahoma, Texas, Georgia, and Wisconsin). Eighty schools elected to participate. Of these, 68 submitted sufficient data and were judged typical enough to be included in the final study. These 68 schools included 37 elementary schools, 10 junior highs and 21 high schools.

There were four sections in the questionnaire. In part 1, the respondent provided school name and address, the grade levels in the school, and the number of students. In part 2, the respondent was to provide the total number of items in each of the Dewey Decimal segments of the collection (000, 100, 200 . . .). Questions in parts 3 and 4 asked library media specialists to identify general and specific emphasis collections, if there were any, and the total number of items in each of these subject collections.

A computer program written in BASIC by May Lein Ho analyzed the data. The program generated a collection map and a collection chart for each school (see tables 1 and 11 as examples). A sample collection map for a typical school is shown in table 1.

Table 1 maps a collection into three segments:

1 The size of the total collection, graphed horizontally at the base of the map.

2 General emphasis area collections which generally support courses of study, mapped vertically on the left. In this case, animals and folklore & fairytales are charted.

3 Specific emphasis areas which generally support units of instruction, mapped vertically on the right. In this collection there are specialty collections for dinosaurs, frontier and pioneer life, and Indians of North America.

The collection map below shows collection strengths of an elementary library media collection in terms of size. Collection quality is not pictured on the sample map but can be measured as described in the previous article. Social studies, science and literature have been emphasized in this collection. There are enough materials about Indians to merit a superior rating; this school, therefore, might be recognized by other schools in the district as a source for supplementary materials.

Table 1
Collection Map

School name:
Number of students: 597
Total collection: 8,289
Number of total collection items per student: 13.88

	Number of items	Number of items per student
General Emphasis Areas:		
1. Folklore & fairytales	305	.5108
2. Animals	263	.4405
Specific Emphasis Areas:		
3. Dinosaurs	53	.0887
4. Frontier & pioneer life	79	.1323
5. Indians of North America	150	.2512

Note: All numbers charted in items per student

Creating the Collection Map Scales

Three of the major purposes of the study were to establish the
scales for the collection map segments, to give the scales reli-
ability, and provide a comparative picture across many schools.
For the total collection graph running horizontally at the base of
the map, the national standard of 40 items per student was used as
a guide. Five incremental and judgmental labels were selected to

denote progress in building collections: "Mediocre," "Making
Progress," "Good," "Excellent," and "Exemplary." All segments
of the collection were to be charted in items per student. Table 2
shows the five labels and the number of items designated for each
label.

Table 2
Scale for the Total Collection Graph

Label	Items/student
Mediocre	0–7.9
Making progress	8–15.9
Good	16–23.9
Excellent	24–31.9
Exemplary	32–40.0

The creation of labels and scales for emphasis areas was more difficult since there was no standard or professional judgment in the
literature to call upon for guidance. Four labels were chosen as
indicative of emphasis area size: "Fair," "Good," "Superior," and
"Exemplary." All of the emphasis collections in the participating
schools were pooled to create the scales. Since there were two
types of emphasis areas, general and specific, two pools were
created. Each of the emphasis area collection sizes was divided
by the number of students in each respective school and then
pooled for comparison.

These results revealed a tremendous difference between the largest
and smallest emphasis collection sizes. Usually, a graphic scale
would be divided into equidistant intervals for charting. In this
case, however, such an equidistant scale proved inadequate.
Therefore, the emphasis size figures were divided into four quartiles, and the resulting numbers of items per student became the
scale intervals. Table 3 shows the emphasis area scale intervals.
In order to generalize the scales and make them practical for general usage, the scales were rounded as shown in table 4.[4]

Comparison of Total Collection Sizes across Schools

After collections for all participating schools were charted and
mapped, the resulting data were analyzed across the schools. As

Collection Mapping: The Research

Table 3
Emphasis Collection Quartiles (Actual)

	General Areas	Specific Areas
Number of areas indicated	258	204
Mean items per student	1.11	.19
Largest number of items per student	15.62	2.05
Lowest number of items per student	.01	.01
1st quartile	.27	.08
2nd quartile	.56	.14
3rd quartile	1.13	.23
4th quartile	15.62	2.05

Table 4
Rounded Emphasis Collection Quartiles

Labels	General Areas	Specific Areas
Fair	00–.30	00–.10
Good	.31–.60	.11–.15
Superior	.61–1.20	.16–.25
Exemplary	1.21–7.00	.26–2.00

shown in table 5, the average collection size ranged from 8,372 in elementary schools to 18,306 in high schools.

When compared with the national recommended standard of 40 items per student, the greatest number of elementary schools (14 schools) were in the range of 16 to 23.9 items per student, with the rating of "Good," while most of the participating junior high and senior high schools were in the range of 8 to 15.9 items per student with the rating of "Making Progress." Table 6 reports the number of schools in each of the rating categories.

Table 5
Average Collection Size, Number of Items Per Student, and Average Emphasis Area Size of the Participating Schools

Level	No. of Schools	Avg. No. of Students	Avg. Coll. Size	No. of Items per Student	Avg. Size of Emphasis Areas
Elementary	37	432	8,372	21.16	2,680
Junior High	10	891	12,521	16.31	2,803
High	21	1,257	18,306	15.79	3,571

Table 6
The Number of Collections in Five Size Categories

Level	Mediocre	Making Progress	Good	Excellent	Exemplary	Total
Elementary	0	10	14	11	2	37
Junior High	0	6	2	2	0	10
High	1	12	8	0	0	21

Scale: Mediocre   =   0–7.9   items/student
       Making Progress =   8–15.9 items/student
       Good   = 16–23.9 items/student
       Excellent   = 24–31.9 items/student
       Exemplary   = 32–40   items/student

Comparison of Emphasis Collections across Schools

The collection mapping technique provided a unique way of comparing the strengths of collections across schools. Library media specialists were asked to identify emphasis collections which were defined as "topical collection segments larger than a 'typical' school might have." Library media specialists in the 68 schools identified 462 emphasis collections. After eliminating duplication and standardizing terminology, there were 134 discrete emphasis collections identified. Collections related to social science, science, reading and literature predominated. Table 7 itemizes the emphasis areas identified in the study.

Table 7 is instructive because it shows the overlap, breadth, and frequency of emphasis collections built by school library media specialists. Overlap of collections, including topics such as states, Indians, animals, and folklore & fairy tales, indicates the most common units of instruction in the country which are supported by library media resources. On the other hand, topics which are unique to one of the 68 collections give an idea of collection breadth. Schools that have large collections in Renaissance history, costume, horticulture, etc., are important in resource-sharing networks. These are the collections which could be shared effectively among the schools within a network. Resource sharing is advantageous among schools if collections are diverse. Table 7 indicates that if these 68 schools were linked, they would have a tremendous pool of materials upon which to draw. If the schools

Collection Mapping: The Research

Table 7
Emphasis Collections Reported in Participating Schools

Area Name	Frequency	Area Name	Frequency
1. SOCIAL SCIENCE	134	2. SCIENCE	112
US history (general)	20	Animals	44
States	17	Astronomy	11
Indians of North America	14	Science (general)	8
World War I & II	8	Computers	6
Countries	7	Earth science	6
Blacks	6	Biology	5
Holidays	6	Physical science	4
Civil War	5	Insects	3
Geography/travel	5	Mathematics	3
Presidents	4	Medical science	3
World history	4	Plants	3
American government	3	Zoology	3
Economics	3	Botany	2
North America	3	Diseases	2
Middle Ages	2	Geology	2
Political science	2	Anthropology	1
Revolutionary War	2	Archeology	1
Social science (general)	2	Construction	1
US history-20th century	2	Horticulture	1
Colonial America	1	Industry	1
Congress	1	Invention & inventors	1
Crime & criminals	1	Natural history	1
Death education	1		
Explorers	1	3. READING	85
Frontiers & pioneers	1		
Pioneer days	1	Folklore & fairytales	22
Political election	1	Picture books	10
Renaissance history	1	Beginning reading	9
Social interaction	1	Biography	9
Social problems	1	Fiction	9
Sociology	1	High/low reading	6
Theodore Roosevelt	1	Children's authors	5
Travel	1	Award-winning books	4
US geography	1	Jokes & riddles	2
US foreign policy	1	Mystery & detective stories	2
US history—1856–	1	Science fiction	2
US history (The West)	1	Animal stories	1
Women	1	Historical fiction	1
		Language arts—junior great books	1
		Scientific biographies	1
		Young adult authors	1

in the study were to weed their collections so that they matched the curricula of their schools, then table 7 would be a true reflection of curriculum areas of the United States which were well supported by library media resources. As it is, table 7 only indi-

Collection Mapping: The Research

Table 7 (*continued*)

Area Name	Frequency	Area Name	Frequency
4. LITERATURE	41	8. SPORTS	12
Poetry	12	Sports	7
Mythology	6	Games	3
Shakespeare	6	Ball games	1
American literature	5	Recreation	1
Drama	4		
American poetry	2	9. VOCATIONAL EDUCATION	10
American authors	1		
American plays	1	Agriculture	1
Authorship	1	Careers	9
English literature	1		
Short stories	1	10. HOME ECONOMICS	7
Theater	1		
		Cookbooks	4
5. ART	20	Food	2
		Home economics	1
Art	5		
Music	4	11. PROFESSIONAL COLLECTION	5
Crafts	2		
Drawing	2	Prof. coll. (general)	4
Art—Western	1	Teacher aids	1
Cartoons	1		
Colors	1	12. PSYCHOLOGY	5
Costume	1		
Handicraft	1	Exceptional children	2
Painters & painting	1	Applied psychology	1
Puppets	1	Child development	1
		Para-psych. & psych.	1
6. HEALTH	13		
		13. REFERENCE	2
General health	4		
Nutrition	3	Reference (general)	2
Drugs	2		
Alcohol	1	14. LANGUAGE ARTS	1
Fitness	1		
Personal growth	1	Creative writing	1
Sexuality	1		
		15. RELIGION	1
7. LANGUAGE	12		
		Religion (general)	1
English language	3		
Dictionaries	2	16. MISCELLANEOUS	1
Foreign languages	2		
German	1	Controversial knowledge	1
Grammar	1		
Latin	1		
Linguistics	1		
Sign language	1		

cates what emphasis collections schools currently own. Sometimes a school will invest in an emphasis collection and then the curriculum will change. In this case, the library media collection and the curriculum will be mismatched.

To summarize table 7, the emphasis areas were combined further into central curricular subjects and ranked. Table 8 gives these rankings.

An analysis of table 8 reveals that emphasis areas dominate in social studies, in collections dealing with reading and literature, and in science. These are the curricular areas which will be served best by the "typical" school library media collection. The data also suggest that there is a tremendous bias built into the collections of school library media centers toward certain segments of the curriculum. High frequency of collections in topics such as states, Indians, poetry, animals, astronomy, and picture books show these biases. A comparison of topics missing on the list but included in a school's curriculum would indicate neglect in the collection-building policy. In this case, the library media specialist might make an analysis of the reasons for collection overlap and collection neglect.

Table 8
Number of Emphasis Areas Grouped According to Curriculum Topics

Curriculum Topics	Total No. of Areas Mentioned	No. of Discrete Areas
Social sci.	134	38
Science	112	22
Reading	85	16
Literature	41	13
Art	20	11
Health	13	7
Language	12	9
Sports	12	4
Voc. ed.	10	2
Home ec.	7	3
Prof. coll.	5	4
Psychology	5	2
Reference	2	1
Lang. arts	1	1
Religion	1	1
Others	1	1
Total	462	134

Collection Mapping: The Research

Library Media Collection and National Selection Lists

The second major component of the research study was to compare the collections of the 68 participating schools with the nationally recognized selection lists: *Elementary School Library Collection, Junior High School Library Catalog,* and *Senior High School Library Catalog.*

The purpose of the Brodart *Elementary School Library Collection,* according to the editor, is to "serve as a resource to assist in the continuous maintenance and development of existing collections, . . . to implement elementary school curricula, and to be of interest and appeal to elementary school-aged children."[5] However, the editor warns: "While the list offers recommendations for elementary schools in a wide variety of settings and at differing levels of collection development, it remains the work of the library media specialist to adapt any basic list to local needs, to select for special curricular projects, and to keep the collection fresh through continuous evaluation and judicious weeding."[6]

The editors of the Wilson lists make little reference to purpose or function of their list in the current edition, but the 1957 edition of *Standard Catalog for High School Libraries* stated the purpose as follows: "to provide a list of books, both fiction and nonfiction, whose usefulness in senior and junior high schools is vouched for by a representative group of experienced librarians and specialists in literature for young people . . . hence the books entered in the Catalog may be said to be of tested usefulness."[7]

The current editions of the recommended lists contain titles which are considered representative in many topical areas, but some areas predominate. Table 9 lists the percentages of materials in each of the Dewey Decimal classes.[8]

In a practical sense, table 9 suggests that a library media specialist might use the national list percentages as purchasing guidelines. A number of specialists have had such purchasing targets, but such a practice has dubious value. It is, however, helpful to compare a school's collection against the standard list as a preliminary step in collection mapping. The library media specialist who is new to a collection might create a chart like table 10 to assist in the identification of emphasis collections.

Table 9
Recommended List Percentages

Dewey Area	Elementary	Junior High	High
Ref.	1.82	3.00	3.00
000	0.82	1.59	1.32
100	1.08	1.82	1.81
200	1.08	1.10	1.71
300	5.09	10.63	13.74
398.2	6.11	0.00	0.00
400	0.80	1.40	1.87
500	10.29	11.55	4.60
600	6.70	9.73	7.15
700	6.31	13.65	7.93
800	2.50	1.84	13.85
900	5.45	13.45	15.89
B	3.47	10.12	12.60
Fic.	23.52	15.27	9.42
SC	1.13	2.35	2.61
Easy	15.87	0.00	0.00
Period.	1.64	0.50	0.50
Prof.	6.32	2.00	2.00
Total	100.00	100.00	100.00

Interpretation: 1.82% of the titles included in the elementary list are reference materials.

The library media specialist examining table 10 would examine the Reference section, 500s, 900s, Biography, and Easy sections first in order to identify emphasis collections. The total collection chart, however, would not help identify emphasis collections that would span several Dewey classes.

When all the schools in the study were compared to their respective national list, some interesting data were generated. Table 11 compares all the elementary collections in the study to the *Elementary School Library Collection* percentages.

Table 11 shows that more than 62 percent of an average elementary school's library holdings were in four categories. These categories in ranking order were: Fiction (21.20%), Easy (18.22%), 500s (12.91%), and 900s (10.31%). When compared to the recommended list percentages, an average elementary school maintained more materials in 900s, 500s, and easy sections than the recommended list. Practically, this means that the national list is not as helpful in some areas as it might be. For example, a library

Collection Mapping: The Research

Table 10
Total Collection Chart

School name:
Number of students: 597
Total collection: 8,289
Number of total collection items per student: 13.88

Dewey Area	Recommended List Percentage	Should Have	Actually Have	Discrepancy	Likely Emphasis Area	Areas That May Need Purchase
Ref.	1.82	151	259	108	*	
000	0.82	68	86	18		
100	1.08	90	39	−51		
200	1.08	90	56	−34		
300	5.09	422	407	−15		
398.2	6.11	506	305	−201		*
400	0.8	66	110	44		
500	10.29	853	1112	259	*	
600	6.7	555	499	−56		
700	6.31	523	516	−7		
800	2.5	207	247	40		
900	5.45	452	981	529	*	
B	3.47	288	496	208	*	
Fic.	23.52	1950	1343	−607		*
SC	1.13	94	61	−33		
Easy	15.87	1315	1641	326	*	
Period.	1.64	136	19	−117		*
Prof.	6.32	524	112	−412		*

media specialist who needs hundreds of easy books to assist beginning readers will find very little help in the list. The specialist would also need additional bibliographies to develop the 900s and 500s collections further.

The Brodart list contained more materials in the areas of the Professional collection, 398.2s and Fiction than the schools in the study. This means that library media specialists needing to build large collections in these areas could use the recommended list to good advantage.

Table 12 compares the collections in the junior high schools of the study with *Junior High School Library Catalog.*

In the junior high school collections, the top ranking categories were: Fiction (26.96%), 900s (14.54%), and 500s (10.75%). Table 12 indicates that the fiction collection in an average junior

Collection Mapping: The Research

34

Table 11
Distribution of Collections—Elementary Schools

Dewey Area	Percentage in School Collections	Recommended List Percentage	Difference in Percentage
Ref.	1.72	1.82	−0.1
000	1.02	0.82	0.2
100	0.54	1.08	−0.54
200	0.61	1.08	−0.47
300	6.58	5.09	1.49
398.2	3.43	6.11	−2.68
400	0.73	0.8	−0.07
500	12.91	10.29	2.62
600	6.29	6.7	−0.41
700	5.84	6.31	−0.47
800	2.67	2.5	0.17
900	10.31	5.45	4.86
B	5.23	3.47	1.76
Fic.	21.20	23.52	−2.32
SC	0.62	1.13	−0.51
Easy	18.22	15.87	2.35
Period.	0.28	1.64	−1.36
Prof.	1.71	6.32	−4.61
Total	99.91	100.0	

Table 12
Distribution of Collections—Junior High Schools

Dewey Area	Percentage in School Collections	Recommended List Percentage	Difference in Percentage
Ref.	6.27	3.0	3.27
000	1.05	1.59	−0.54
100	0.81	1.82	−1.01
200	0.85	1.1	−0.25
300	8.46	10.63	−2.17
400	1.28	1.4	−0.12
500	10.75	11.55	−0.8
600	7.71	9.73	−2.02
700	8.61	13.65	−5.04
800	3.82	1.84	1.98
900	14.54	13.45	1.09
B	5.60	10.12	−4.52
Fic.	26.96	15.27	11.69
SC	1.52	2.35	−0.83
Period.	0.35	0.5	−0.15
Prof.	1.40	2.0	−0.60
Total	99.98	100.00	

high school was significantly larger than that suggested in *Junior High School Library Catalog.* The reference collection was also larger. On the other hand, *Junior High School Library Catalog* provided many more titles in 700s, Biography, 300s, and 600s.

Table 13 compares the collections of the 21 high schools in the study to *Senior High School Library Catalog.*

In the high school collections, more than one-third of the collection in the average high school was devoted to two categories: Fiction and 900s. The third largest section was the 300s. The schools had significantly more materials in Fiction, 500s, and Reference, while the recommended list was stronger in Biography and 800s.

The comparative analysis of percentages and topical areas shows that schools build different collections than these lists recommend. While definite conclusions about the reasons for these differences are difficult, a few possibilities might be suggested. If library media specialists who are close to their teachers and the curriculum are buying for the needs of their schools, then their collection strengths should serve as models that publishers and national list editors should follow. In many instances, this might

Table 13
Distribution of Collections—High Schools

Dewey Area	Percentage of Total Col.	Recommended List Percentage	Difference in Percentage
Ref.	5.82	3.0	2.82
000	1.5	1.32	0.18
100	1.7	1.81	−0.11
200	0.97	1.71	−0.74
300	12.44	13.74	−1.3
400	1.46	1.87	−0.41
500	8.5	4.60	3.9
600	7.63	7.15	0.48
700	7.83	7.93	−0.1
800	9.88	13.85	−3.97
900	15.99	15.89	0.1
B	6.12	12.60	−6.48
Fic.	17.12	9.42	7.7
SC	1.69	2.61	−0.92
Period.	0.45	0.5	−0.05
Prof.	0.89	2.0	−1.11
Total	99.99	100.00	

be true. For example, it seems clear that the Brodart list provides an overabundance of titles in folklore and fairytales and that biography collections are overly strong. The art and biography collections in the junior high list are extra large. The high school list emphasizes biography unduly. However, the large proportion of fiction in the junior high and senior high collections is worrisome —not because large fiction collections are bad, but when funds are limited, it would seem wiser to concentrate purchases in non-fiction areas. It seems that the lingering emphasis on building a collection for "supplementary reading" is still being followed. Some hard questions deserve attention: Are library media specialists building collections out of sync with the "video generation" of youth as well as their curricula? Are editors of national lists following too many publishing trends rather than curricular trends?

Conclusions and Recommendations

The two purposes of this study were: 1) to test the collection mapping technique and establish confidence in its picture of a school library media collection, 2) to compare collections of materials in schools with nationally published recommended lists.

The research provided evidence that collection mapping is a viable technique for collection analysis and collection management. The mapping procedure is simple enough to be done without extensive training, and the resulting graphic representation of a collection is not only a representation of collection strengths but also charts strength against a national sample of schools. Three important collection segments were identified and charted:

1 The size of the total collection is charted against the national standard of 40 items per student. This charting represents collection size and breadth.

2 The size of general emphasis collections which support courses of study is charted and compared to collections of the same type in the nation.

3 The size of specific emphasis collections which support individual units of instruction is charted and compared to collections of the same type in the nation.

The collection-mapping technique, as tested in this study, works well in schools with student populations of 500–1000. Schools

Collection Mapping: The Research

with smaller and larger student bodies would need altered scales. Large schools should have fewer items-per-student needed for excellence ratings and small schools would need more items per student.

The study gave added evidence of the breadth and depth of school library media collections in the country. The library media specialists identified 431 emphasis collections in the 68 schools, covering 134 distinct topics. These collections provide sufficient diversity to support a network of resource sharing. The potential to share collections as evidenced in this study is one of the nation's richest untapped resources.

The 1975 national guidelines recommend a minimum of 20,000 items or 40 items per student for every school over 500 students. The guidelines also state that library media specialists in large schools may not wish to achieve the ratio of 40 items per student. The schools in this study, which are typical according to national statistics, show that elementary schools have more items per student but smaller collections than secondary schools. In this study, the average collection size for elementary schools was 8,372; for junior highs, 12,521; and 18,306 for high schools. More research needs to be done to establish minimal collection sizes, not just for total collections but for collections to support units of instruction and courses of study. Perhaps size standards for curriculum blocks would be a direction to investigate.

One glaring oversight of the 1975 guidelines was the lack of guidelines for building professional collections. Very few of the schools in this study had sizeable professional collections. In some districts, library media specialists noted that professional materials were held at the district level rather than the school. In others, these collections were very small or nonexistent.

The second aspect of the study, the comparison of collections to nationally published lists, provided new insights into the composition of the recommended lists versus actual collections of materials. Library media specialists generally build collections to support supplementary reading and subject-oriented collections which serve social studies, literature, and science. It is not surprising that school library collections and services only appeal to a part of the total curriculum and teaching staff in a school.

The study clearly pointed out that school library media specialists build different collections than national lists recommend. Na-

Collection Mapping: The Research

38

tional lists contain emphasis collections which have developed over a period of time and which thus need re-examination in light of current school curriculum. The orientation of national lists toward what publishers publish is as troubling as the narrow focus of the collections in schools.

A major problem of collection building in schools became very evident during the study. Library media specialists complain that high quality materials are not available in many curricular areas. Publishers tend to publish high-demand materials. Standard lists include what is published. Review periodical coverage includes mostly fiction and other literary works. Library media specialists buy from recommended lists and reviews. This cyclical phenomenon needs revamping if school collections are to support the total curriculum.

All segments of the market need to cooperate if change is to take place. Library media specialists need to map their collections and create acquisition targets that match their curriculum—then channel their money into those areas. Publishers of national lists need to re-assess their lists regularly and adjust the scope to truly reflect the curriculum of the nation's schools. H. W. Wilson, for example, hasn't yet discovered that audiovisual media are as basic as books in an educational institution. Review periodicals need to have better coverage of curricular materials.

The present research has called into question the role of a nationally published list of "basic" materials for school library media centers. Perhaps there will always be a need for a core list of titles needed in most schools, but considering the current curricula and the availability of computer technology, perhaps it is time to suggest that both H. W. Wilson and Brodart rethink the "raison d'être" and the methodology that go into creating their publications. Perhaps core titles and emphasis collections could be made available on floppy disks on a subscription basis and/or online. Such a database could be under continuous revision and could expand far beyond the current efforts toward core materials only. If books continue to go out of print as has happened in the past few years, the value of a printed list is questionable.

Perhaps the best advice to library media specialists that this research offers is to build collections in topical segments rather than just buying "things." Nationally-published core lists may be

Collection Mapping: The Research

useful in building a few basic materials in a topical area, but building strength and depth into a collection requires a different approach.

Notes

1 Lois Winkel, ed., *The Elementary School Library Collection: A Guide to Books and Other Media,* 14th ed., (Williamsport, PA: Bodart Co., 1984).

2 Gary L. Bogart and Richard H. Isaacson, eds., *Junior High School Library Catalog,* 14th ed., (New York: The H. W. Wilson Co., 1980).

3 Gary L. Bogart and Richard H. Isaacson, eds., *Senior High School Library Catalog,* 12th ed., (New York: The H. W. Wilson Co., 1982).

4 One school in the 4th quartile had an emphasis collection so large (15.62 items per student) that it was eliminated when the quartiles were rounded.

5 Lois Winkel, p.v.

6 Ibid.

7 Dorothy Herbert West and Marion L. McConnell, eds., *Standard Catalog for High School Librarians,* 7th ed., (New York: The H. W. Wilson Company, 1957), p.v.

8 Readers will note that none of the Wilson lists has a separate reference or professional collection. The researchers had to estimate the size of these collections through careful analysis of each Dewey section.

Collection Mapping and Collection Development

William Murray, Marion Messervey, Barbara Dobbs, and Susan Gough

The Aurora, Colorado Public School District had media collections which gradually expanded as it developed from a district of one elementary school and a single high school during World War II to its present size in 1985 of 25,000 students served by 29 elementary schools, 7 middle schools, 5 high schools and a technological center. These are located in a typical suburban community of 180,000 people on the eastern boundary of Denver, Colorado.

Aurora was a farming center for many years, but this changed when several military bases were located nearby during and after World War II. Thus, it became a bedroom community serving the bases, the growing industry of Denver, and the Stapelton International Airport.

The Aurora Public School District is traditional in its approach to media. Starting with the high school libraries in the 1930s, the district added junior high libraries after World War II. As information demands expanded, elementary services were initiated in the 1950s, first with volunteer staff and then with professional personnel in the late 1960s. In the 1970s, the concept of the media center began to emerge. It was not until the 1980s, however, that the philosophy of a service center was developed, one uniquely designed to give maximum service to schools, not just a warehouse patterned after public libraries.

In the early 1980s, it was determined that using the national norms for collection size, as reflected in publications of AASL and AECT, was no longer a valid method for assessing media collections. Certainly these quantitative figures gave part of the picture. But some principals and media specialists were keeping materials on the shelf merely to maintain high book counts when good weeding was what was needed. It was thought that large collections, regardless of quality, were important to accreditation efforts. As schools went from phase one counts to phase two and three

Collection Mapping and Collection Development

counts, more frequently the question was being asked, What is the meaning of numbers in terms of improved learning?

Interest in methods of collection evaluation was high when the district first encountered the collection mapping technique developed by David V. Loertscher. Schools at the high school level had already proceeded with a collection analysis developed from the work done in the Mesa Valley, Colorado District under the leadership of Sara Parker, then with the Colorado State Library and now head of the Montana State Library. Her technique had been influenced by the work of Ellen Altman in collection development for public libraries and by that of Joseph P. Segal in a rationale for weeding known as the CREW method.

After reviewing Loertscher's collection mapping, it was determined that this technique had much to offer in its simplicity of approach, emphasis on cooperative follow-up activities, and production of a graphic interpretation of the collection in order to improve understanding.

The Aurora library media group determined to adopt collection mapping, but to refine the technique to meet local educational demands. These changes included adjusting recommended percentages for each Dewey area of the collection and adjusting base collection size requirements. Loertscher's Dewey percentages were based on grade configurations of K–6, 7–9 and 10–12. Aurora schools are split, K–5, 6–8, and 9–12. Loertscher's base collection sizes are based on AASL/AECT standards. The Aurora library media specialists have questioned these figures from the beginning, especially the nonprint recommendations and the method of tabulation. With this in mind, a more pragmatic count was determined for the base collection with the 11–12 item-per-student range listed as "good" and rising to "exemplary" when more than 21 items per student were in the collection (see the collection maps later in the article). With these changes in place, all schools were asked to take part in the collection mapping project, and all agreed to participate.

Support for the project developed in the following stages which were vital to its success:

1 Library media specialists became convinced of the need to adopt better ways to look at a collection rather than just using the old bromide "professional judgment."

2 Support was forthcoming from district level supervisory personnel (called level directors in Aurora).

3 Principals were asking for more definitive collection building guidelines.

4 Workshops conducted by David Loertscher which included all media personnel and key district leaders were held.

5 Key committee work was done on release or paid time.

For reporting this study, three typical collection mapping projects are described, one each at the elementary, middle school and high school levels. The reporting library media specialists include: Marion Messervey, Hinkley High School; Barbara Dobbs, East Middle School; and Susan Gough, Laredo Elementary School. These professionals have also provided leadership at their respective grade levels for the collection mapping project.

The three library media specialists have varying levels of experience with collections. At the high school level, Marion Messervey has been with the library media center since 1967 and has had a considerable impact on collection development. At the other extreme, Barbara Dobbs started her job at East Middle School just a month before the collection mapping was done. Susan Gough had had several years of experience with her collection before the mapping project began. Barbara Dobbs found collection mapping a good way to get to know a collection quickly, while the other two discovered specifics about their collections they had not found in their day-to-day work.

The three schools also provide a good middle ground for looking at library development in the Aurora Schools. All are "midlife" schools in the system. They are not among the oldest, built in the 1950s, or the newest, built in the 1980s, but just in between. One might call them middle-aged.

The collection mapping project in Aurora is only complete in its first phase. The follow-up phase—the use of curriculum involvement forms, presentations to principals and other administrators, meetings with faculty, budget and collection targeting strategies— is to be implemented in the future. Without follow-up, the project will become a dead issue very quickly.

Case studies of three schools' encounters with collection mapping follow.

Collection Mapping and Collection Development

William C. Hinkley High School

Hinkley High School opened in the fall of 1963 as a three-year high school (grades 10–12) and remained so until 1974 when the middle school concept was adopted by the district. This resulted in the ninth grade being incorporated into all high schools in the district.

The school draws from a wide attendance area, which results in the students coming from broad socioeconomic backgrounds and situations ranging from low income to middle and some relatively high-income families. Many of the students' parents are members of the military, and this magnifies the transiency of the student population. Students live in suburban residential developments, mobile home courts, rental housing, and some on farms. Ethnic minorities comprise approximately 20 percent of the student population.

Student enrollment has ranged from over 2,000 students to a present enrollment of approximately 1,700 students. Residential development within the attendance area has stabilized for the present. This, combined with the opening of a new high school in the fall of 1983, accounts for the drop in student enrollment.

The collection for the building's library media center was established along traditional and somewhat conservative lines with a strong consciousness of the curriculum. It still reflects this emphasis, notably in the content areas of English and social studies. Extensive purchases were made to implement the literature courses. In the early years of the school, there was a strong aerospace education program that received emphasis.

Funds for the library media center came both from the district and ESEA Title II grants. The federal funds enabled the media center staff to open and continue to develop the collection from a much stronger position than would otherwise have been possible. However, spending for the collection has been declining for the past ten years.

Throughout the years, as the curriculum has changed, the collection has maintained a strong curricular emphasis. Much of the basic subject content has remained the same, but the course format has changed. This has influenced the development of the collection. For a period of several years, biological science,

Collection Mapping and Collection Development

American history and upper level English offerings were developed around quarter classes. This necessitated a more concentrated effort to supply materials for these courses, which was done at the expense of collection development in subject areas such as industrial arts, business, physical education, upper-level science courses, and mathematics. In the past three years, year-long survey or semester courses have replaced many of the quarter course offerings. This change in itself presents a challenge to collection development.

The Aurora high schools were introduced to collection mapping following participation in a collection evaluation project which focused on the collection of data that would provide indicators of quality rather than just quantitative assessment. These included factors of currency and utilization as well as count. Therefore, collection mapping provided a second picture of collection strengths and weaknesses.

Analysis of the collection map (see figure 1) for Hinkley High School shows a high degree of concentration of resources for the

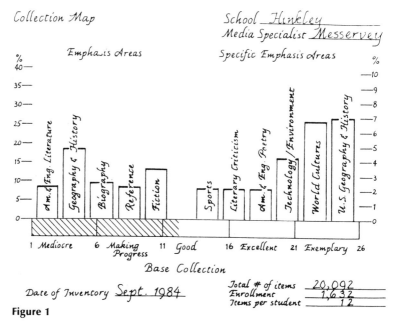

Figure 1

Collection Mapping and Collection Development

two broad curricular areas of English and social studies. Emphasis areas exist in American and English literature. This area is complemented by two other emphasis areas—biography and fiction.

The specific emphasis area section of the map verifies the literature concentration showing strong collections in poetry and fiction. The American and English fiction collections deal almost entirely with the treatment of the literature from a historical and critical viewpoint.

The reference collection is larger than standard percentages would declare appropriate. This section reflects the early purchasing patterns combined with the slotting of some books into this category, which validly should not have been there. Progress has been made in removing some of these books. The mapping process has focused attention on the need to reevaluate materials and collection segments.

The geography and history areas of the social studies curriculum have received much attention as the collection has developed. The materials relating to world cultures are excellent and the United States geography and history collection draws heavily not only on the books in the 900s but also materials in the 300s.

Technology and environment, one of the science units, draws materials from several Dewey categories and has been a particularly strong resource for students. Students' recreational interests are also well served by the sports collection.

The collection mapping technique has been revealing and rewarding. It has provided a view of segments of the collection for analysis and comparison with curricular needs. Another help has been to recognize the crossover of disciplines. For example, the art department would be lost without books on botany, zoology, geography, and several other areas.

One of the challenges presented by collection mapping is the realization that the library media collection may contain many valuable but unused materials. Should these materials be weeded? Should efforts to entice teachers to use the materials be stepped up? Should more active involvement in curriculum planning be sought?

There is a definite need to build long-range collection development plans tied to the district's seven-year plan for curriculum revision and text adoption. In addition, budgeting requests need to be coordinated with collection development targets. Perhaps the best aspect of the whole technique has been the building of a strong decision support system for the future.

East Middle School

East Middle School opened in 1965 as a junior high school but was converted to a middle school when all Aurora Public School junior highs were changed to the 6–8 grade level format in 1974. Over the years, student enrollment has fluctuated from a high of 1,400 students to a low of 850. East has the largest attendance area of the district, encompassing the northeastern edge of the city.

Students come from a variety of homes, including single-family subdivisions, mobile home parks, condominiums, apartments, farms, and ranches. The attendance area includes Buckley Air National Guard Base, which results in a highly transient student population. Students come from lower-middle-class neighborhoods, and the number of minority students has been increasing steadily.

The library media center collection was developed in two distinct portions, the print collection and the nonprint collection. The emphasis then was directed toward placing a mini-public library in a school setting, with very little effort to match materials to the curriculum. During this time, paperbacks were being touted as the only type of books for school libraries to purchase. The librarian at East believed in this approach, and, for a while, East had the largest paperback collection in the district. There are still multiple copies of paperback fiction in the collection.

The collection is relatively old with an average publication date of 1970. The average publication date of circulated materials is 1973. The number of items per student is, by most standards, adequate. (See figure 2.) But after determining the average age of the collection, the numbers do not appear as impressive, considering that a large portion of the materials should be weeded.

When comparing East's collection with other middle school collections in the district, several contrasts are evident. East's collection is strong in fiction and art/recreation. The other middle school collections reflect stronger curriculum support. Two emphasis areas identified in East's collection, fairy tales and poetry

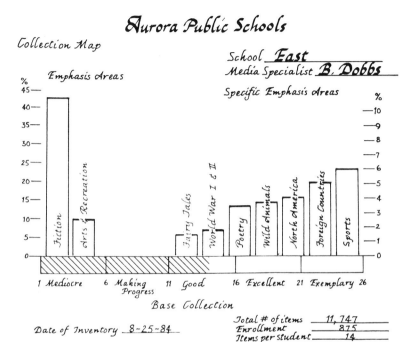

Aurora Public Schools

Collection Map

School **East**
Media Specialist **B. Dobbs**

Emphasis Areas

Specific Emphasis Areas

Base Collection

Date of Inventory 8-25-84

Total # of items ___11,747___
Enrollment ___875___
Items per student ___14___

Figure 2

support very short units in the language arts curriculum. Since many of these volumes are unattractive, the mapping suggests that these collections should be weeded and de-emphasized in future collection development. The remaining emphasis areas identified such as wild animals, North America, etc., all support areas extensively studied by students at East.

The major finding at East was that the collection does not support enough of the curricula to expect extensive use at the present time. While the fiction collection shows great strength in numbers, the majority of books are old and unattractive and do not capture the interest of the students, who have a history of being nonreaders. At one time, East had both print and audiovisual professionals in the library media center. When the staff was reduced to one person and the print professional left, collection development, particularly in the fiction area, suffered.

The collection mapping project certainly has dispelled the theory that a prescribed number of items per student equates with a quality collection. Materials must be relevant to the curriculum and of interest to the students if they are worthy of a place on the shelves.

The local budget for print and nonprint materials has not varied appreciably over the last ten years at East. Given inflation and enrollment fluctuations, the collection has not fared well. Recently, the district has made a commitment to a three-year collection renewal project. The use of the collection map and qualitative measures are now contributing to pinpointing collection targets. In addition, they provide a ray of hope for improving the future impact of the library media center.

Laredo Elementary School

Laredo Elementary School opened in 1966 and currently educates approximately 400 students from middle and lower-income neighborhoods. Many parents have employment in the military or other governmental agencies so the student population tends to be transient. As parents gain in economic wealth, they tend to move from the area. In addition, the size of various ethnic populations is increasing.

The library media collection at Laredo (see figure 3) was started mostly from remainder materials purchased from various vendors. The idea was to build a supplementary reading collection fast and then concentrate on curricular materials. This collection development policy has now been reversed.

The collection map for Laredo is typical of the elementary collections in Aurora. The age of the collection is one of the more interesting facts. A six-year difference exists between materials that circulate (1974) and the average age of all materials in the collection (1968). There are a large number of children's classic fiction and easy titles, including fairy tales which have older copyright dates. These items are essential to the collection, but provide a skewed number in consideration of age. In the curricular areas, newer materials are preferred by students and teachers, as expected.

The total collection size is 16.8 books per student, which charts on the collection map in the "excellent" range. In years of tighter budget restraints, the uncertainty of removing items without being able to replace them tends to keep some older materials on the shelves. Intensive weeding should bring the collection down to

Collection Mapping and Collection Development

approximately 11 volumes per student and just into the "good" range on the collection map—a figure which would be much more realistic.

The emphasis areas as charted reflect the students' interests and reading habits. Twenty-five percent of the collection is in the fiction section, including popular children's authors and titles. The Laredo student population has a strong interest in the outdoors, and students read extensively in the natural sciences. In addition, the adoption of a new science curriculum and the expenditure of considerable amounts of money in regular and ECIA funds have increased the science emphasis area to 12 percent of the collection.

The easy materials collection makes up the final general emphasis area, accounting for 20 percent of the collection. This emphasis area is the result of deliberate collection development by the library media specialist over the past six years. The purchase of many classics, as well as multiple copies of popular titles, supports the primary grade reading curriculum and the interest of students

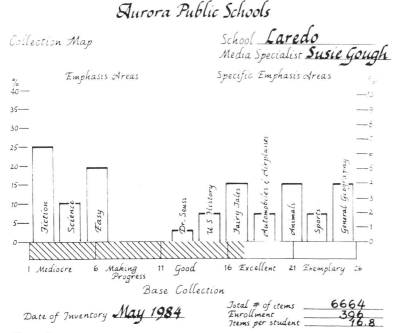

Figure 3

in pleasure reading. This emphasis area is also heavily used by a wide age-ability range of students in kindergarten through fourth grade.

The specific emphasis areas are directly related to the school curriculum. For example, the study of animal life is covered at every grade level in science and the 4 percent of the collection devoted to animals is an asset to these studies. However, when only a few items are available on one animal and several grade levels use the same titles, the result is overuse and overexposure. It is evident that many more titles in the area of animals are needed if interest is to be sustained.

After analysis of the collection map, several collection targets have been identified to receive budget emphasis in the next few years. These include world geography, technology, and physical science topics. Since instruction in reading is a major thrust in the elementary curriculum, a wide variety of materials in both phonetic decoding and comprehension will be ordered.

Conclusions

The collection mapping process has helped the Aurora school administration and library media staff take a thorough look at the collection strengths and weaknesses in the district. The philosophies that collections should support the curriculum and that teacher-library media specialist cooperation in collection development is essential have been underscored.

In addition to collection mapping, measures on collection ages were taken. This led to an entire district program of collection renewal, starting with a focus on the reference and periodical collections. The development of recommended lists for these two collections has assisted library media specialists in evaluating their collections and in the selection process.

Another result of the entire collection evaluation effort has been a concentration on systematic weeding. Initially the CREW method was used. In addition, the guidelines for weeding school collections as presented by the Calgary Board of Education have gained acceptance.*

---

* Calgary Board of Education, "Weeding the School Library Media Collection," *School Library Media Quarterly* (Fall 1984).

Collection Mapping and Collection Development

Another benefit derived from collection mapping has been to focus the library media specialists' attention on the interrelationships of the print and nonprint components of their collection.

Collection mapping has been just one piece in a (total) long-range program for collection renewal in the Aurora schools. Using it has not only focused collection building efforts, but through the various workshops held, has helped administrators become more aware of the special role of library media centers in education. The results of the entire project should pay dividends for a number of years to come.

Effect of Certain Reporting Techniques on Instructional Involvement of Library Media Specialists

Retta Patrick

Introduction

The idea that school library media programs should become a part of—not be apart from—a school's basic instructional program is not new. The concept has been promoted in library literature for more than 25 years. The 1960 standards moved in this direction.[1] The 1975 standards, *Media Programs: District and School,* further emphasized library media center involvement with curriculum and learning:

> The media program exists to support and further the purposes formulated by the school or district of which it is an integral part, and its quality is judged by its effectiveness in achieving program purposes . . . the more sensitively it responds to the curriculum and the learning environment, the better the media program. . . . A basic component of all media programs is the human interchange among the media staff, between media staff and administrative staff, between media staff and teachers, and most of all, between media person and student.[2]

How does the library media practitioner go about translating the sometimes difficult terminology of national standards and research studies into practical solutions to such problems as: Who are we? What should we be doing? Where do we begin? How do we find the time for new responsibilities? How do we sell this "new instructional role" to others—especially to classroom teachers and administrators?

This article will present the attempts of Pulaski County Special School District to synthesize library media standards with the research findings and ideas of some educators in the profession. Some assumptions and related problem areas concerning library media center instructional involvement will be identified. Specific

decisions and actions relating to library media specialists' attempts
to promote library media center instructional involvement at
various levels will be discussed. Finally, certain techniques will
be presented for measuring, documenting, evaluating, and reporting these actions aimed at increasing instructional involvement.

Some Basic Assumptions

Recent library media literature, educational research, and the experience of practitioners support the following assumptions about
library media center instructional involvement:

1 Library media program effectiveness is ultimately measured by
its effect on student learning.

2 Student learning tends to be more effective when library skills
are taught and applied to a specific classroom need.

3 Library media specialists who are aware of the curriculum and
specific unit topics to be taught tend to provide more effective resources and instructional support.

4 Classroom teachers who are aware of available library media
resources tend to plan more learning activities involving library
media center resources and library skill instruction with classroom
units.

5 Instructional involvement of the library media program tends to
increase as communication and planning between classroom
teachers and library media staff increase.

The transition from developing the theory of library media center
instructional involvement to putting it into practice has been slow
for several reasons. Some skeptics simply reject this idea. There
are many reasons, they say, why it "can't be done." The excuses
of "not enough time" and "lack of understanding by teachers and
administrators" are among those most often given by library media
specialists for not assuming an active instructional role. The traditional library responsibilities of selecting, ordering, organizing,
circulating, and managing library media center resources can
easily fill the available time. Torn between the current demand
for assuming shared accountability for student learning and ful-
filling the day-to-day operation of the library media center, there
is a tendency to choose the latter. Don Ely, in describing the

Effect of Certain Reporting Techniques
on Instructional Involvement of Library
Media Specialists

"identity crisis" faced by today's school library media specialist, wrote, "it seems easier to retreat to the more comfortable roles of the past than to reach out and embrace an uncertain future.[3]

Ely attributes the "identity crisis" to conflicting role expectations emanating from at least three sources: 1) self-perceptions of the library media specialists, 2) perceptions of others—teachers, administrators, students, parents, and the general public, and 3) job descriptions that present expected or ideal behavior.

Mohajerin and Smith found significant differences in perceptions of the media specialists' role among college and university media educators, practicing media specialists, principals, and teachers.[4] Their literature search reveals a "massive shift in the role expectation for the school media specialist resulting from a major change in school philosophy and organization: the transition from a teacher-centered perspective to a learner-centered one."[5] In summarizing their research, Mohajerin and Smith concluded that "without an intensive educational effort involving fellow workers, the emergent role of the media specialist is at best only partially perceived or understood and its actual performance is inhibited."[6]

From Theory to Practice: What Should We Be Doing?

During the ten years since the publication of *Media Programs: District and School,* a number of library media educators (and a few practitioners) have attempted to translate the theory of library media center curriculum involvement into some common sense, practical approaches. One of the most effective of these approaches, developed by David Loertscher, involves the use of a "Taxonomy of LMC Instruction Involvement."[7] Each of its levels builds on the successful involvement of the previous levels. By using the Taxonomy as a guide, a library media specialist can develop confidence and competence while responding to student and teacher requests for library media center resources. Building on the successes and the growing credibility developed with teachers and students, specialists can move from the reactive to the proactive levels of the Taxonomy. As knowledge of the curriculum grows, the library media specialist feels comfortable with promoting higher levels of instructional involvement.

Liesener, in *A Systematic Process for Planning Media Programs,* cited major decisions that today's library media specialists must make.[8] They must decide how to use limited resources (e.g., time) to benefit the most students; determine what to do and what not to do; and then decide how to justify these decisions. He wrote that simply responding to demands as they are made often results in haphazard, inconsistent service and inefficient, ineffective use of time and other resources. Liesener proposes an alternative response—the application of management techniques developed by business. This involves systematic planning and evaluation of library media programs as a basis for improving services to students and teachers.

While the extensive planning, programming, budgeting system (PPBS) proposed by Liesener may not be realistic for adoption by the single-professional building staff, certain elements of his approach can be applied successfully. Time has already been cited as a limited resource in library media programs. In Liesener's opinion, library media specialists generally have a great deal of flexibility and potential control over the way they use their time. He wrote that substantial increases in both efficient and effective use of time are possible, even in the early stages of collecting data and planning changes.[9]

The ideas of both Loertscher and Liesener have been applied as the library media specialists of Pulaski County Special School District, Arkansas, have moved toward increased instructional involvement. Also considered was the strong evidence that role perceptions of classroom teachers and administrators must be changed if instructional involvement was to be effective.

Ten Years of Program Building: 1970–1980

Since the early 1970s, Pulaski County Special School District has placed strong emphasis on development of instructional programs based on student needs. The district-wide commitment to a student-centered curriculum has been ideal for the growth of library media instructional involvement.

In 1970, there was a professional librarian in each secondary school and 11 professionals in 30 elementary schools. By 1975, this had grown to full-time professionals in every school plus clerical help. Full-time clerical staff were available in every school by 1980. This excellent staffing ratio came by degrees, starting with progress in the largest schools, tying staff increases to accreditation, and adding personnel when new schools were constructed.

The cliche that "success breeds success" proved to be true, as library media specialists in the district moved from merely reacting to requests to initiating action. This effort was stimulated by inservice activities which began in the early seventies. These monthly inservice meetings, held on released time, provided forums to develop the philosophy that the instructional role was a top priority. Many sessions had to be planned to work out details of instructional involvement since library media specialists had not been taught this role in library school.

There was a point at which the library media specialists had gone as far as they could without involving principals and teachers. The approach was to select one teacher per building for joint planning experiments. As each experiment was completed, the project's success was shared with the principal. At this point, joint inservice programs were held for library media specialists and principals. Information was developed for principals from monthly reports, which included brief data on involvement in instruction. The idea was to show that library media specialists were teachers and that they supported the teaching process.

Finding the time to plan with teachers became a problem, especially in larger schools and at the secondary level. A 45-minute daily planning period, scheduled district-wide at the end of the school day, offered the opportunity for teacher-media staff planning at the elementary level. Secondary schools, however, had no common school-wide planning time scheduled.

Monthly action taken at the district level responded to building level needs. Staff development for library media specialists was planned to strengthen their competencies in such areas as public relations or communication with administrative and instructional staff; instructional design and curriculum planning; and effective management techniques: managing time, streamlining routine tasks, developing goals, and setting priorities. Joint inservice sessions for principals and library media staff focused on promoting a better understanding of the library media center curriculum role and ways in which the two groups could work together to implement this role. The need for three-way continuous communication among library media specialists, classroom teachers, and principals was strongly emphasized.

The effectiveness of district-wide staff development was obvious. Principals showed increasing support for the library media center curriculum role—a vital prerequisite to effective instructional involvement. Through the principals' support, library media program decisions became a shared responsibility of the school staff. Library media program advisory committees at the building level were formed in each school to provide feedback on the effectiveness of existing library media center resources and services, to determine priorities on what to do and what not to do, and to plan improvements. Each spring, input from this group was used in the development of goals and a specific plan of action for improving library media center instructional involvement the following year.

Austerity and the 1980s

Creativity among educators tends to flourish in times of austerity. The Pulaski County District, along with many school systems in the country, experienced cuts in funding in the early 1980s. Staff reduction and elimination of programs became imminent. Only programs that could demonstrate their direct impact on student learning were considered essential. At this point, the years of building credibility for library media program instructional involvement were rewarded. Both library media center staffing and programs remained intact, even when cuts in other instructional areas were made.

Something positive can come from adversity. Anticipating further cuts, the library media staff in the district became even more aware of the necessity for documenting their instructional activities and keeping others informed about their role in teaching and learning. The tendency to pat themselves on the back for having survived was quickly replaced by a strong commitment to create more effective and efficient library media programs—to give the best service possible to the most students. This called for improving their overall knowledge of the curriculum and of the unit topics to be taught, and for creating ways to communicate and plan with as many classroom teachers as possible. To accomplish these goals, library media staff in Pulaski County District set about finding better techniques for measuring, documenting, evaluating, reporting, and justifying future action toward improving library media center instructional involvement.

Effect of Certain Reporting Techniques on Instructional Involvement of Library Media Specialists

A Research Plan for Accountability

The management techniques developed by the district since 1982 were planned and implemented as the library media staff searched for solutions to the following problems:

1 How can school library media specialists increase a) their awareness of unit topics to be taught in the classroom and, b) teacher awareness of available library media resources, services or instruction to support classroom units?

2 Can a concerted effort by library media specialists to promote library media center involvement in instruction result in an increase in one or more of the following?

● The number of teacher contacts initiated by library media specialists to promote library media center resources/services

● The number of classroom teacher requests for library media center resources and services

● Communication between the library media specialist and classroom teachers to plan library media center curriculum related activity

● The integration of library media center resources, activities and skill instruction with classroom units

The first step was to encourage library media specialists in every building to become knowledgeable about the curriculum and unit topics to be taught. Principals were asked to provide the library media center with a copy of adopted textbooks. A curriculum survey form, designed by a junior high media specialist to secure advance notice of unit topics to be taught, was adapted for use throughout the district. These approaches were implemented in 1982. With the encouragement of district and building-level administrators, teachers were asked to respond to the simple survey form by listing unit topics (and textbook pages) to be covered during the coming month (at the elementary level) or the nine-week grading period (at the secondary level). This communication now provides media staff with advance notice of upcoming unit topics and gives lead time for locating library media resources to support unit topics.

When completed curriculum forms are received, the library media specialists scan available textbooks to improve their knowledge of the scope of the unit and the specific subject to be covered. Prepared with their overview of the unit in the textbook and with some suggestions for supporting resources and activities, the staff then respond to the curriculum surveys. Face-to-face contacts are initiated as often as possible to clarify unit approaches or objectives. These contacts often lead to higher levels of instructional involvement, as library media specialists encourage teachers to include skills for using library media resources as a part of unit objectives.

The second step was to document the new communication between the library media specialist and the teacher and to share this progress with school administrators. It was thought that the very act of reporting regularly to a school administrator concerning instructional involvement would be a catalyst to further involvement. A systematic plan was developed, and is now used, to initiate communication and planning with teachers. This plan involves the evaluation of the quantity and level of current library media center contacts and the development of action plans for improvement. Documentation of existing curriculum-related contacts involves the use of a Checklist of LMC Instructional Involvement. This checklist, a quick-tally sheet, roughly follows Loertscher's LMC Taxonomy. Library media staff use this instrument to document 1) their responses to individual teacher requests for library media center resources (Taxonomy Levels 1–4), and 2) their efforts to promote library media resources and plan instructional units involving library media center resources and activities (Taxonomy Levels 5–10). A sample checklist is shown in figure 1.

While it is impossible to remember each teacher contact, only a few minutes once or twice each day are required to recall and record which teachers have made requests and which have been contacted by the library media staff. The time spent in tallying the use of the library media center by teachers cannot be justified unless the results are used for planning future action. Checklists have proved to be useful in evaluating the level and frequency of library media instructional involvement with each teacher. Data from the checklist have pinpointed some problem areas. The tendency for library media staff to spend a large part of their time giving service to a few teachers quickly shows. If staff are devoting most of their time simply responding to teacher requests, this is also obvious. Individual teachers who make few or no re-

Effect of Certain Reporting Techniques on Instructional Involvement of Library Media Specialists

Teacher's Name (Subject/Grade Level)	LMC Response to Teacher Requests			Media Specialist/Teacher-Communication/Planning/Cooperation				
	Materials; Information	Equipment; Production	Resources for Classroom Unit	MS Promotion Resources/Ideas	MS/T Contact (2-5 min.) Communication Scheduling	Formal Planning Instructional Unit (20 min.)	MS Teaching Integrated LMC Skills	

School_____   Pulaski County Special School District
Checklist: LMC Instructional Involvement   Dates:_____

Figure 1

quests are also easily identified. Once these gaps in existing services are noted, action can be planned.

Data from the checklist have been used for three basic purposes:

1 As a self-motivator for library media staff to initiate future contacts with individual teachers and to promote library media center instructional involvement at higher levels

2 As documentation for reporting current library media center activity to building principals and other staff

3 As justification for future action toward planning program improvements at both the building and district levels[10]

At the end of the 1983–84 school term, library media staff in each school analyzed the data from monthly checklists and reports of library media center activities. This documentation of program activities was used in working with building-level library media center advisory committees and principals to evaluate existing programs and set goals and priorities for the 1984–85 school year.

District-wide, library media program involvement in the curriculum at various levels showed a large increase over the preceding year. However, there was evidence that some teachers still were not using library media resources effectively to support their instruction. As district-wide library media program goals were developed from the compiled building-level goals, major emphasis was placed on improving communication techniques between library media staff and teachers. As building-level staff discussed the successful approaches they had used to ensure frequent contacts with teachers, one common thread was evident in each approach: high priority was given to making time for contacting teachers to promote and plan library media center instructional involvement.

A Second Try

What would happen then if a concerted effort were made by the library media specialist in each school to improve communication with teachers? Documented efforts in this area for the 1983–84 school year were analyzed by building level staff. Reports from personnel who had been most successful indicated that a concerted effort to promote library media center resources and services would result in an increase of one or more of the following:

1 The number of contacts initiated by the library media specialist to promote library media resources/services

2 Classroom teacher requests for library media center resources and services

3 Jointly-planned instructional units by the library media specialists and teachers

4 Integration of library media center resources, activities and skill instruction with specific classroom topics.

To test the above hypothesis, the following goal was set for each library media specialist during October 1984: to improve library media center instructional involvement by increasing efforts to promote, communicate, and plan with classroom teachers and other staff. Each school developed its own plan of action toward reaching this goal. Specific action planned by the library media specialist was listed, along with supporting action to be taken by the principal, library media center advisory committee, and other staff.

As action plans were implemented, requests for library media center resources, teacher contacts initiated by library media staff, and communication/planning sessions were tallied on the check-

lists. At the end of October, data were analyzed from each
school. Library media specialists evaluated their efforts toward
following the action plan prepared at the beginning of the month.
Reports from each school were submitted to the district director of
library media services for comparison with the month of October
1983.

Analysis of Data and Results

When results of the "concerted efforts" were compiled at the district level, complete data were available for 39 of the 49 schools
in the district. Data were not included for schools in which there
had been a change in library media professional staff, or for which
documentation of library media center responses/contacts was not
available for both the months of October 1983 and October 1984.

A comparison of combined library media center activities for the
39 schools during October 1983 and October 1984 strongly supported the assumption that specific action by the library media
specialist to promote library media center instructional involvement would have positive results in one or more of the stated
areas. By placing a high priority on promotion efforts and making
the time to contact individual teachers, the average number of
contacts per teacher more than doubled at both the elementary
and secondary levels. The bar graph in figure 2 shows the marked
increase resulting from efforts at each level. Average contacts per
teacher each month at the elementary level increased from 4.4
contacts in October 1983 to 9.5 contacts in October 1984; at the
secondary level, average contacts per teacher increased from 1.42
in October 1983 to 4.87 contacts in October 1984.

There is strong evidence that a direct correlation exists between
increased promotional efforts by the library media staff and an increase in the number of requests by teachers for library media
center resources and activities. The bar graphs in figure 3 show
this increase at both levels. Average responses per teacher during
the month almost doubled at the elementary level from 8.68 responses per teacher in October 1983 to 16.22 responses per
teacher in October 1984; at the secondary level, average responses per teacher more than doubled, increasing from 3.40 in
October 1983 to 8.03 in October 1984.

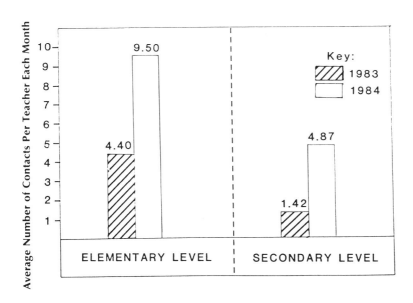

Comparison of Library Media Specialists'
Contracts to Promote Library Media
Center Resources

October 1983: October 1984

Figure 2

Anecdotes from Library Media Specialists

Documentation of increases in both the number of teacher requests for library media center resources and the number of staff contacts to promote their instructional involvement is further supported by library media specialists' evaluations of their progress during October 1984. Following are excerpts from six media specialists reporting on different techniques used and/or their observations about the effectiveness of these approaches:

**Comparison of Library Media Center
Responses to Teacher Requests
October 1983: October 1984**

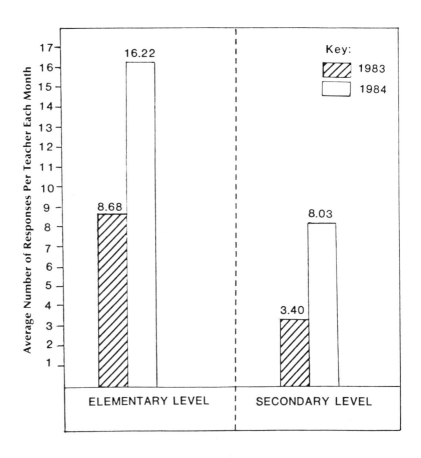

Figure 3

I think the most beneficial step to increasing library media instructional involvement . . . has to be the distribution and response to the curriculum survey sheets. When I handed these
out, only five were returned. After responding to these, I then
would take a planning period to visit teachers by grade level,

asking them what they would be studying. . . . The following day we would gather materials from them in response to their needs. Most of the staff have been very receptive and most appreciative. I have also felt more knowledgeable about what is "going on". . . . Visiting each teacher every week becomes more and more difficult. I seem to get tied to the library media center during planning period helping teachers preview computer materials and planning with those who come to ask for help. If I don't make one team during the week, I just pick up there the next week. . . . None of the success our program enjoys would be possible if not for the total cooperation we receive from our principal. She continually supports the library media center program by carrying out the steps listed in her action plan. (Mary Van Cleve, Mabelvale Elementary)

Seeing every staff member every week was too much and did not allow me any time in the center to take care of those people who came in after school for additional help. . . . I have decided to see each staff member every month because that is when their units change. . . . I really do enjoy knowing what each teacher is doing on a more personal basis. I have had several opportunities to help in casual ways as well as directly aiding instruction. I feel much more effective at my job as a result of this modified checklist, because I now have a definite plan to communicate with staff members each month. Before I did this kind of plan, I usually spent more time with those instructors who were more "media-minded." Now I am much more balanced in my approach to the whole staff. (Suzie James, Oakbrooke Elementary)

A library media center planning schedule was developed, providing for a 20-minute planning session with each teacher and the instructional specialist. A total of 17 sessions were scheduled. Appointments with 12 teachers were met. Staff development meetings (local and district), parent-teacher conferences, late buses, and illness were all factors preventing the completion of the schedule. Additional sessions were held with two teachers. . . . I planned with the instructional specialist, resource teacher and four classroom teachers (grades 4–6) to provide for increased library media center instructional involvement in the science and social studies areas for resource students. Social studies activities have begun for fifth and sixth

Effect of Certain Reporting Techniques on Instructional Involvement of Library Media Specialists

year students and one group of fourth year students have begun science activities. The activities include simple research and media production in an effort to reinforce concepts presented in the classroom. The biggest obstacle seems to be the scheduling of students—It has really been difficult to find a time to get together. (Marsha Hamm, Lawson Elementary)

As a result of one-on-one meetings with teachers, we provided them with materials to supplement or complement their units, made suggestions about other ways we could help them, and began to work on specific skill activities to be completed at a later time. . . . Every teacher received written communication in the form of a "Media Memo" informing them of new materials, periodical articles of interest, or other items we thought would be of benefit. Many of these materials were requested immediately. . . . At staff meetings the principal promoted the use of the library media center—our materials, facilities, and expertise—as a means of making teaching more effective. (Carolyn McFarland, Mabelvale Junior High)

The chemistry teacher and library media specialist worked together identifying science indexes that advanced students needed to learn to use. The objective was to introduce students to sources . . . to retrieve information from college libraries, either for independent use or when they attend college. The library media specialist designed folder activities using these sources. (Wanda Jones, North Pulaski High)

The in-depth planning for library media center activity with the two teachers from the social studies department . . . has gone quite well, with plans and activities almost completed for scheduled times in November. As a result of the plans for the activities with the social studies teacher, I formed an outline for state reports. . . . This outline was shared with all social studies teachers. . . . We planned a reference lesson to accompany this state report. . . . I also have planned with the teacher for the expansion of her social studies activities beginning in November. (Margaret Monk, Sylvan Hills Junior High)

Conclusions

The quantity and quality of library media program instructional involvement can be increased with persistent effort over a long period of time. It began to happen in the Pulaski County Special School District when the library media practitioners accepted the ideas of such educators as Loertscher, Liesener, Ely, and Callison. Practical approaches were found for promoting the instructional role, documenting action, and involving others in making decisions about the way library media center resources and staff time should be used to benefit the most students.

Time continues to be a problem. As instructional involvement increases, there is a growing need to find more effective ways to manage time and other limited resources. It has been almost ten years (1976) since Liesener wrote: " . . . the choice is clear-cut: manage or be managed—plan or accept the planning of others—communicate the meaning of media programs to clients and administrators or accept poor use, confused client perceptions of the program, arbitrary and unexpected budget cuts. . . ."[11]

In a time of declining budgets and increasing demands for accountability for student learning, library media specialists can no longer survive on excuses.

Notes

1 American Association of School Librarians, *Standards for School Library Programs* (Chicago: American Library Association, 1960).

2 American Association of School Librarians and Association for Educational Communications and Technology, *Media Programs: District and School* (Chicago: American Library Association, 1975), p. 4.

3 Donald P. Ely, "The Role of the School Media Specialist: Some Directions and Choices," *Journal of Research and Development in Education* 16 (Fall 1982):33–36.

4 Kathryn S. Mohajerin and Earl P. Smith, "Perceptions of the Role of the School Media Specialist," *School Media Quarterly* 9 (Spring 1981):152–63.

5 Ibid., p. 153.

6 Ibid., p. 155–56.

7 David Loertscher, "The Second Revolution: A Taxonomy for the 1980's," *Wilson Library Bulletin* 56 (February 1982):417–21.

Effect of Certain Reporting Techniques on Instructional Involvement of Library Media Specialists

8 James W. Liesener, *A Systematic Process for Planning Media Programs* (Chicago: American Library Association, 1976), pp. 1–2.

9 Ibid., p. 85.

10 For practical approaches to data collection and its use as documentation for planning and justifying library media program action, see Daniel Callison, "Justification for Action in Future School Library Media Programs, *School Library Media Quarterly* 12 (Spring 1984):205–211.

11 Liesener, p. 86.

Personality and Communications Behaviors of Model School Library Media Specialists

Barbara Herrin, Louis R. Pointon, and Sara Russell

Profile: Bright, capable, somewhat reserved yet projecting an aura of warmth and enthusiasm, confident, stable, not dependent on the group, attentive, able to communicate effectively.

Who is pictured? A physician? An airline attendant? A teacher? A psychologist? Look again. The profile is a *librarian*—a *school library media specialist* today!

During the past two decades libraries have been transformed into media centers and now even into information/communication centers. Yet the stereotype of the introverted librarian has lingered—even among those in the profession. Over the years, several studies have been conducted to ascertain the accuracy of the stereotype and, until recently, the findings showed the picture sketched remarkably true to life.

The librarian's self-image communicates a powerful message to patrons. Only recently has the interaction of this stereotypical personality picture on the actual communication process in the library been considered.[1] On examining past studies of librarians, Black notes: "The implications for communications are not auspicious. Effective operations involving considerable autonomy require confident, capable people working mainly at the adult level with efficient, productive and appropriate communication abilities. There is little evidence of these abilities in these people."[2]

Is Black's concern for the communications effectiveness of librarians warranted—especially among school library media specialists today? Are there patterns—of personality and of communication—that distinguish or contribute to the effectiveness of library media specialists? These were the questions that prompted an in-depth study of exemplary school library media specialists. The purpose of the study was threefold: 1) to check the personality descriptions of model school library media specialists against the stereotypical librarian described in earlier research; 2) to describe the communications abilities of the model library media specialists using a structured observation and interview approach; and 3) to examine the methodology of the study and make recommendations concerning its use in expanded studies or other environments.

Methodology

The methodology used for the study was a modified case study approach. Successful school library media specialists were nominated by their peers (representatives from the school library media director's organization, the State Department of Education, and the presidents of professional library organizations in the state). Five of the candidates most frequently named were chosen for intensive investigation. The communications activities of these model media specialists were observed in the actual library settings and categorized by trained observers using a classification scheme with similarities to the Flanders Interaction Analysis Scale.[3] In addition, each media specialist completed a series of four inventories (16 PF [personality], Tennessee Self-Concept Scale, Study of Values, and the Bienvenu Interpersonal Communications Inventory) and participated in an interview that concentrated on personal perceptions of success and communications abilities.

Review of the Literature

Before comparison between today's model library media specialist and the stereotypical librarian is possible, it is necessary to fill in the details of past pencil sketches of personality. Black summarizes the touchstone studies of Bryan[4] and Douglass,[5] noting that the librarian of the period (1940s) was conscientious, conservative, conforming, adverse to change, introverted and not social, overly critical, careful of his impression on others, not a leader, and interested in people in an intellectual rather than personal way.[6]

Ten years later, Morrison described the academic librarian as intelligent, self-assured (a change), lacking greatly in supervisory qualities, and lacking even more in initiative.[7] Furthermore, there was little evidence that the librarian knew or understood himself with any clarity.

Personality and Communications Behaviors
of Model School Library Media Specialists

Another ten years later, McMahon,[8] Clayton,[9] Sladen,[10] Presthus,[11] and Plate[12] confirmed many of the earlier descriptions. Presthus observed that "the vast majority of librarians have a tenuous commitment to change and innovation,"[13] and as Black restated: "Most seemed to feel that brains rather than a pleasing personality would get them farther ahead, an indication not only of their priorities, but of a certain naivete and lack of political skills already evidenced in Douglass' work 20 years earlier."[14]

It is well known that our educational system is suited to teaching technical and conceptual (cognitive) skills. Less is known about how professionals are influenced in their education when it comes to the development of human relations/communication skills. However, these skills are considered important performance elements for managers. In a 1981 article on selecting library managers and leaders, Eggleton[15] defined three types of skills that should be examined and considered requisite in candidates for middle and higher management: human relations skills, technical skills, and conceptual skills. He asserted:

> While every manager requires expertise in all of these areas, the degrees of each skill needed will vary with management level. . . . As one moves from lower to higher levels of management, the need for technical skills decreases and the need for conceptual skills increases. At the middle management level, human relations skills are the most important . . . (although) human relations skills are dominant at all levels.[16]

Yet, evidence indicates that librarians do not consistently choose to recognize communication or human relations skills as important to success. For example, Plate and Siegel surveyed MLS graduates concerning library education and career satisfaction.[17] They found graduates "perceived their personality as being the main reason for success and good interpersonal relationships as being third after environmental opportunity."[18] However, when lack of success was evidenced, personality became less important and lack of interpersonal skills fell to tenth place (perhaps a case of crediting themselves with success and blaming others for failure?).

Interestingly, librarians tend to differ from other professionals in their views of success. For those graduating with an MBA, success is defined as job position, administrative level, salary, and scope of authority (i.e., upward mobility). Eggleton discovered that librarians in technical and public services were not high in need for achievement.[19] That there was, however, some need for affiliation suggested a desire for communication. Plate also found that librarians were ambivalent about upward mobility, and he concluded that librarians do not perceive a need for power and seem to lack managerial and political skills. Can the lack of skills in these areas be attributed in part to a lack of interpersonal communications skills as well?

Though the personality and communications image of librarians is lackluster, more recent studies offer some bits of optimism. For example, DeHart[20] conducted a study of communication skills among library school students which suggested "that courses in communications and human relations could be effective among those with high marks coming into library schools."[21]

A study of personality by Kenney and Kenney used the 16 PF to compare librarians and teachers.[22] The study revealed librarians to be less rule-bound than their teacher counterparts, more imaginative and more unconventional, yet tender-minded and less group oriented. Fortune and Gibbons, using the same instrument to correlate personality to success, found "superior media graduates" to be bright, assertive, venturesome, imaginative, experimenting, and self-sufficient.[23] They also were more outgoing than the norm.

A very recent study by Charter examines six school library media programs—including the media specialist—in depth.[24] The 16 PF was utilized to describe the personalities of the librarians and found them to be outgoing, bright, stable, mildly assertive, happy-go-lucky, somewhat conscientious, venturesome, tender-minded, trusting, moderately imaginative, forthright, self-assured, experimenting, group-dependent, controlled and average in terms of expression of tenseness.

Thus, the professional literature portrays librarians in two ways— the stereotypic introvert and the more assertive extrovert. This study attempts to look specifically at successful school library media specialists, to ascertain their place on the continuum, and to delineate personality and communications abilities that may contribute to their successes.

Personality Profiles

Classifying the successful school library media specialists according to introversion/extroversion proved difficult. The 16 PF

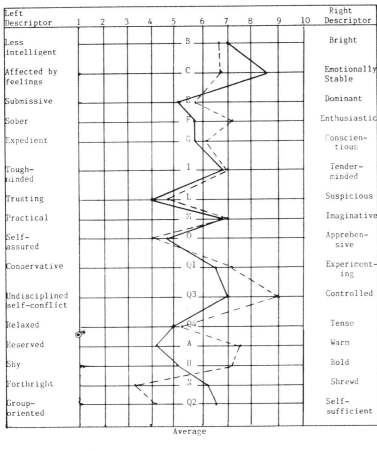

Left Descriptor	1	2	3	4	5	6	7	8	9	10	Right Descriptor
Less intelligent					B						Bright
Affected by feelings					C						Emotionally Stable
Submissive					E						Dominant
Sober					F						Enthusiastic
Expedient					G						Conscientious
Tough-minded					I						Tender-minded
Trusting					L						Suspicious
Practical					M						Imaginative
Self-assured					O						Apprehensive
Conservative					Q1						Experimenting
Undisciplined self-conflict					Q3						Controlled
Relaxed					Q4						Tense
Reserved					A						Warm
Shy					H						Bold
Forthright					N						Shrewd
Group-oriented					Q2						Self-sufficient

Average

_____ Herrin/Pointon Study   N = 5

- - - - - Charter Study   N = 6

Figure 1: Comparison of Composite 16 PF Scores

revealed the media specialists in this study to be similar to those in the Charter study in many ways, as noted in figure 1. However, in direct contrast to the Charter study (and more like the early Bryan/Douglass models), these model school library media specialists were found to be introverted/reserved and somewhat shy. To confound the picture, the personal observations of the researchers did not confirm reserved/introverted behavior in the actual school/library setting. (Was the library setting familiar and comfortable, allowing for more ease in interacting?—or were the

Table 1
Comparison of Personality Traits of Traditional Librarians and Model Library Media Specialists

Traditional Librarian	Model Media Specialist	Agree/Mixed/ Disagree	Sources of Evidence
Conscientious (5,30)*	Average in dichotomy between expedient and conscientious	D	16 PF
Conservative (5)	Experimenting (29)	D	16 PF
Conforming (5,8)	Not group dependent; self-sufficient	D	16 PF
	More aesthetic—tends toward self-sufficiency (29)		Values**
Adverse to change (5,9,11)	Experimenting "Enjoy variety/change in job" "Liked exploring new ideas/options" (29)	D	16 PF Interviews Interviews
Insecure, lacking confidence, feel inferior (4,26)	Self-assured (7,9)	D	TSC****
Task-oriented vs. people-oriented (20)	"Must take care of routine clerical tasks expeditiously in order to spend time with people"	D	Interviews
	Social orientation		Values
Need for affiliation (23)	Not group-dependent; towards self-sufficiency	D	16 PF
Not creative (8)	Experimenting, towards imaginative High aesthetic (enjoying diversity)	D	16 PF Observations Values
Desiring close supervision (11)	Does not have close supervision	D	Observations
Lacking supervisory/managerial qualities (7,17)	Managers of time/people	D	Observations
Overly critical (5)	Not critical	D	Observations
Introverted (4,5,11,26)	Introverted/reserved Outgoing "Enjoy people" Sense of adequacy in social interactions	M	16 PF Observations Interviews
Not social (4,5)	Somewhat shy, reserved but enjoys people More aesthetic—interested in people	M	16 PF Interviews Values

Table 1 (continued)

Traditional Librarian	Model Media Specialist	Agree/Mixed/ Disagree	Sources of Evidence
Careful of impressions (5)	Not group dependent; self-sufficient	M	16 PF
	Feel a "lack of acceptance" by others		IPCI***
Cautious (9,10)	Shy, controlled towards imaginative	M	16 PF
Lacking in initiative/ leadership potential (4,5,7,10,17)	Experimenting but also somewhat shy and non-assertive	M	16 PF
	Initiated contacts		Observations
	Liked exploring "new" ideas/options		Interviews
	Active, holding leadership positions in school library association at state level		Observations
	Less political		Values
Respecting authority (8)	Toward imaginative as opposed to practical	M	16 PF
	Toward experimenting as opposed to conservative		
	Toward conscientious (rule-bound)		
	Toward shy, restrained, threat-sensitive		
	Good relations with administrators		Observations
Avoiding controversy (8)	Avoiding controversy	A	Interviews Observations
Intelligent (7,29,30)	Intelligent/abstract-thinking	A	16 PF
Controlled (9,10,30)	Controlled	A	16 PF
Not desirous of power/ political skills	Not political	A	TSC
No high need for achievement (23)	Not highly political nor economic	A	Values
Desiring autonomy (11)	Self-sufficient	A	16 PF TSC
Self-assured (7,9)	Toward unperturbed, self-assured	A	16 PF TSC
	High average self-acceptance and sense of personal worth		
	Emotionally very stable, mature, patient, calm		16 PF
	High average self-acceptance (30)		TSC
	Trusting		16 PF
	Self-disclosing (30)		Observations

Personality and Communications Behaviors
of Model School Library Media Specialists

Table 1 (continued)

Traditional Librarian	Model Media Specialist	Agree/Mixed/ Disagree	Sources of Evidence
	Tender-minded (intuitive/sensitive) (28,30)		16 PF Observations
	Neither excessively dominant nor submissive		16 PF Observations

     * Numbers denote study from which descriptor was taken.
    ** Study of Values
   *** Interpersonal Communications Inventory
**** Tennessee Self-Concept Scale

(4) Bryan, 1952	(17) Plate, 1979
(5) Douglass, 1957	(20) DeHart, 1975
(7) Morrison, 1961	(23) Eggleton, 1978
(8) Plate (1970)	(26) Sladen, 1972
(9) Clayton, 1968	(28) Kenney & Kenney, 1982
(10) McMahon, 1967	(29) Fortune & Gibbons, 1981
(11) Presthus, 1970	(30) Charter, 1982

expectations of the job such that interaction was demanded?) Also unlike the Charter study, the model school library media specialists were more astute and shrewd as well as less group oriented. Even with these differences, the two recent studies are quite similar, and both show marked deviance from the traditional introverted and insecure model (see table 1).

Differences from the earlier descriptions are also confirmed through examination of the Tennessee Self-Concept Scale. The composite Tennessee Self-Concept scores (see figure 2) show that the model school library media specialists accept themselves as they are, feel quite adequate as a person (apart from body or relationships), perceive themselves as adequate in social interactions, generally feel valuable as a family member or in relation to their most immediate circle of associates, consider themselves to be morally worthy and are generally satisfied with their religion or lack of it, have a positive self-concept (only 1 of 5 was even slightly below average), feel good about "who they are," consider their behavior consistent with what they believe and say, are average in terms of self-criticism, and are somewhat less satisfied with their physical selves—skills, sexuality, and or appearance (only 2 of 5 were actually below average, but all 5 rated themselves lower in this area).

The Study of Values created by Allport, Vernon, and Lindzey,

Personality and Communications Behaviors
of Model School Library Media Specialists

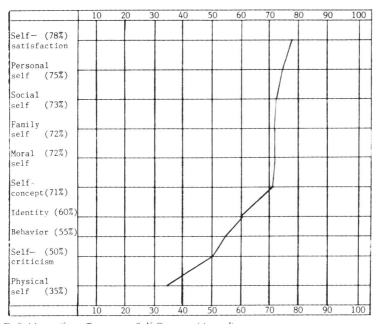

Definitions: (from Tennessee Self-Concept Manual)

Self-satisfaction: reflects general level of self-acceptance or how individual feels
   about the self he/she perceives.
Personal self: sense of personal worth, feeling of adequacy as a person, and
   evaluation of personality apart from one's body or relationship with others.
Social self: reflects a person's sense of adequacy and worth in social interaction
   with people in general.
Family self: reflects one's feelings of adequacy, worth, and value as a family
   member.
Moral-ethical self: describes self from moral-ethical frame of reference—moral
   worth, relationship to God, feelings of being a "good/bad" person,
   satisfaction with one's religion or lack of it.
Self-concept: reflects overall level of self esteem.
Identity: reflects "what I am" or how one sees oneself.
Behavior: reflects "what I do" or the individual's perception of own behavior
   or way he/she functions.
Self-criticism: openness and capacity for self-criticism.
Physical self: reflects person's view of own body, state of health, physical
   appearance, skills, and sexuality.

Figure 2. Composite Scores—Tennessee Self-Concept Scale

evaluates the relative prominence of six basic interests or motives
within the individual personality—theoretical, economic, aes
thetic, social, political, and religious.[25] When compared to the
norms for adult women, the combined scores of the model library
media specialists followed the general profile (see figure 3). Most
strongly evidenced in individuals were the aesthetic and social
motives, suggesting the media specialists are interested in people
and have a desire for form and harmony in their environments and
relationships. Less strong are the economic, political, and theoretical motives, indicating that the library media specialists' motives are more idealistic than practical and that they are less de-
sirous of power and economic success.

Communication Profiles

Creating a personality profile of model media specialists is just one
component of this study; a primary goal is to examine communications styles as an extension of personality. The Bienvenu Interpersonal Communications Inventory gave each library media spe-

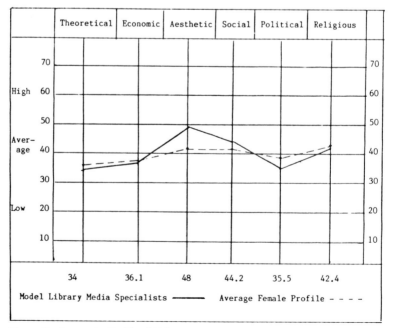

Figure 3: Composite Profile of Values

Personality and Communications Behaviors
of Model School Library Media Specialists

cialist the opportunity to evaluate her own communications effectiveness.[26] The inventory is intended to measure not the content of communication, but rather patterns and characteristics of the communications process utilized by the individual. Patterns in eleven areas are explored: self-disclosure, awareness, evaluation and acceptance of feedback, self-expression, attention, coping with feelings, clarity, avoidance, dominance, handling differences, and perceived acceptance.

The combined results of the inventories showed that four of the five model media specialists felt "good" about their communications abilities with one rating her skills as "average." As figure 4 shows, the model library media specialists consider themselves to be highly aware—of themselves, of the reactions and body language of others, and of how others might be feeling and reacting in an interaction. They feel fairly confident about their abilities to express themselves and be understood and are generally willing to reveal feelings and ideas—expressions of trust and the willingness to listen to and understand the other person. Scores on the avoidance, handling of differences, and coping with feelings ele-

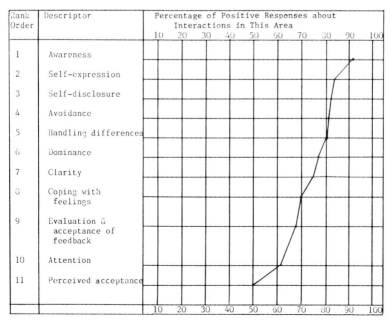

Figure 4: Composite Scores on Interpersonal Communications Inventory

ments show that the model library media specialists are uncomfortable with disagreements, but feel relatively good about the manner in which they are able to resolve them. The lower scores in the areas of clarity and acceptance of feedback may indicate that the library media specialists not only find it difficult to evaluate and accept feedback, but also feel they do not clarify what another means in an interaction often enough. That four of the five library media specialists felt a distinct lack of acceptance by others seems somewhat at odds with their willingness to be self-disclosing. While two of the five considered themselves most attentive, the others admitted that frequently they did not give full attention to another in conversation or merely pretended to listen at times.

Observations

How accurate are self-evaluations? Direct observation of the media specialists at work provided a means of checking. Utilizing a structured observation form suggested by the Bienvenu Interpersonal Communications Inventory and the Flanders Interaction Analysis Scale, each library media specialist was "shadowed" by one of two researchers for four-hour periods on three randomly selected days.

The observational data suggests a number of reasons for the success of the model media specialists. Perhaps the most striking is the tremendous number of interactions (10,944 or an average of 186 per hour). Four of the five library media specialists spent more than three quarters of their time communicating!

Table 2
Time Spent in Oral Communication

Model Library Media Specialist	Total Interact	Approx. Minutes Spent Communication	Total Minutes Observed	% of Time in Communication
#1	3,324	637	720	88.5
#2	2,473	529	649	81.5
#3	2,299	558	720	77.5
#4	1,930	551	720	76.5
#5	918	280	720	38.9

Of course, these figures are affected by the working conditions and schedules of each library media specialist:

Personality and Communications Behaviors
of Model School Library Media Specialists

Table 3
Working Conditions

Media Specialist	School Level	Setting	Teachers	Children/ Young Adults	Clerk	Other Factors
#1	Elem.	Suburban	27	452	1 pt	Classes 5 hrs/day
#2	HS	Rural	19	270	1 pt	Activity sponsor
#3	Elem.	Suburban	26	450	1 pt	Used flexible scheduling
#4	Middle	Suburban	18	340	0	
#5	HS	Urban	88	1,550	1 ft	2 full-time librarians

The following summary of data includes definitions for the categories of behavior observed (see table 4). Note that in contrast to their own evaluations, the library media specialists were observed using attention-giving behaviors far more frequently than any other category of interaction. This attentive behavior included many smiles and encouraging expressions, frequent use of student/faculty names, touching—especially for those who work with younger children, good eye contact, and active listening. An interesting sidelight: the library media specialists whose 16 PF profiles indicated a cool, detached attitude actually utilized the attention-giving techniques more than those who were characterized as warm and outgoing. Thus, the 16 PF may indicate a personal reserve that limits self-disclosure (see #5) while focusing more attention on others.

As might be expected in a profession with information as its core, questioning and information-giving behaviors were utilized with high and approximately equal frequency. Clarifying behavior was used significantly more by two library media specialists—ones who declared that young people seldom have much experience in formulating and expressing their needs adequately. These media specialists suggested a practice of forcing students (with patience, restatements, and careful prodding) to verbalize their needs and questions clearly—a philosophy evidenced in their actions.

Humor was not used excessively by any of the media specialists but was important in setting the tone for many interactions. Library media specialists were quick to see the humor of a situation and smiled frequently to "soften" difficult situations. Those dealing with older youths tended toward mild sarcasm at times—with a positive effect.

Personality and Communications Behaviors
of Model School Library Media Specialists

Table 4
Summary of Observational Data

		% of Interactions by Each Library Media Specialist					% of Total Interactions
Rank Order	Type of Interaction	#1	#2	#3	#4	#5	
1	Attention-giving	50.09	38.21	40.71	25.03	28.76	39.24
2	Questioning	15.52	18.84	20.70	11.92	10.02	16.33
3	Information-giving	11.85	23.25	12.96	11.40	13.94	14.83
4	Clarifying	6.95	4.61	7.87	22.38	19.17	10.34
5	Self-disclosure	3.28	7.28	4.57	14.51	13.73	7.27
6	Humor	3.55	6.67	7.97	3.68	2.72	5.07
7	Dominating	1.41	.89	3.52	7.36	7.08	3.26
8	Praise/encouragement	6.32	.20	1.39	1.61	3.27	2.82
9	Harmonizing	.30	.00	.22	1.19	.11	.43
10	Avoiding	.57	.00	.13	.73	.22	.33
11	Criticizing	.00	.04	.00	.21	.22	.06
		100.02	99.24	100.04	99.84	99.99	99.98

* See table 2 for total interactions for each media specialist.
** Numbers do not total 100% because of rounding.

Definitions:

Attention-giving: showing empathy; accepting others' feelings; recognizing establishing eye contact; acknowledging ideas, feelings; listening
Questioning: asking for information
Information-giving: initiating new ideas; offering alternatives; giving directions; persuading
Clarifying: (information must already have been given) restating; asking for feedback; summarizing; asking for explanation
Self-disclosure: admitting/disclosing feelings or personal information not generally for public knowledge
Humor: joking; laughing at another's joke; making light of a situation
Dominating: interrupting; using authority; asserting superiority; speaking louder; patronizing or condescending; demeaning others' status; telling others what to do in a pushy way; monopolizing conversation
Praise/encouragement: (self-explanatory)
Harmonizing: resolving a conflict; compromising; consensus testing; handling differences; agreeing
Avoiding: blocking; disengaging; breaking eye contact; changing subject; resisting beyond reason; avoiding recognition
Criticizing: attacking; deflating; using barbed comments

Observations affirm the positive stance of the library media specialists toward their own use of dominating behavior. Seldom engaged in by any of the library media specialists, almost all instances of dominating behavior were "using authority" in a manner appropriate for the teaching situation.

From the literature of teaching we know that positive reinforcement and praise are most effective in learning; yet most suprisingly, praise and encouragement were used very little by these model media specialists. If praise was seldom given, did that make it mean more? Was focused attention given instead of praise? If so, was the attention itself sufficient to evoke the desired positive response?

Harmonizing, the resolving of differences with compromise or consensus, was also little used by the library media specialists. Perhaps each had already established a positive rapport with both students and faculty. Furthermore, each acknowledged avoiding controversy if possible—and if not, there was a desire to deal straightforwardly with the problem.

Behavior with negative overtones—avoiding and criticizing—occurred most infrequently. Avoidance behavior happened often because the media specialist was attempting to maintain full attention in conversation with another individual. The media specialists might prefer to avoid conflict, but they certainly did not avoid people. Nor did they choose to criticize: those at the elementary level, not at all; those working with older youths, only rarely. Furthermore, observers noted that the criticisms given were mild in nature.

Thus, actual observation of the interpersonal communications of the model media specialists showed them to be highly responsive and attentive to their patrons, active participants in the information transfer process: both giving and receiving information and willing to clarify to assure clear communication. They were fairly open and self-revealing; they enjoyed a laugh, and were able to harmonize and to exert appropriate authority without dominating. They seldom verbalized praise or utilized negative behavior such as avoidance or criticism.

Interview Results

An "exit interview" offered each of the model media specialists an opportunity to share insights concerning her own perceptions of success and its relationship to personality and communications style. The interview also served as a "check" on the accuracy of both the personality/communications inventories and the observations. An interview schedule was used as a guide for the taped conversations, which were later subjected to a content analysis.

Most interesting was the fact that when asked to identify three reasons for their successes, the model library media specialists offered remarkably similar responses: enjoyment of their work and contact with people—both youths and adults (4/5); and willingness to accept the role of curriculum leader (3/5). Other responses included willingness to change, understanding of children's learning styles, being a good synthesizer, taking the initiative, and longevity in a setting.

In describing what they liked most about their jobs, the challenge of working with a variety of people and topics was mentioned by all five. Other responses included: the ever-changing nature of the job (3/5); viable programs for "educating to more than mediocrity"; and the challenge of keeping the channels of communication open.

Responses to the query "what do you like least about your job?" brought agreement also. Four of the five identified clerical tasks first; the fifth suggested the extensive extra-curricular activities. Other dislikes included: a lack of time to complete tasks; frustration at the inability to provide in-depth assistance to every child; the need to be rigid about necessary rules; circulation and security problems; and long hours.

When asked to describe their own communications styles, the model library media specialists used terms such as "direct" (3/5), "open" (2), "clarifying" (2), "fresh/breezy," "succinct," "capable," and "sublimating of own feelings."

Further exploration of communications styles showed that all five media specialists were uncomfortable with conflict and avoided it when possible. However, though it might cause frustration, each preferred to deal with a conflict directly and privately. Three suggested that in conflicting situations it was often necessary to be able to step back, examine the problem from another's point of view, and be willing to change. Those interacting with older youths stressed treating the individual with dignity—whether student or faculty member. (One media specialist dealing with an urban poor population suggested that avoidance of conflict was an outgrowth of her philosophy that the library media center should provide youth who generally experience great upheaval in their lives an organized way of living and opportunities for peace and quiet.)

All library media specialists agreed that humor was an important element in human communication. None saw herself as a joke-teller, some saw humor as a tension-reliever, but all admitted that being able to see and laugh at human foibles made the job easier. Quotes:

I'd hate to work without it [humor]!

The day passes quicker in a happy atmosphere—and after all, kids are funny!

I look for humor in situations because some of the stuff we have to deal with is so tragic that if you didn't, you'd sit down and cry.

When asked to summarize their professional philosophies, the model library media specialists provided some thoughtful responses:

MS#4: Be open to ideas and willing to learn. Set goals and re-establish them frequently, remembering that learning never stops. Be tolerant of all points of view and of differing levels of ability in students and in teachers.

MS#5: Library media is primarily a helping profession and the library media specialist's role is to work towards developing curricular programs. Spend time on professional tasks. Be assertive about the role and delegate responsibility when possible. Do what is best for the most and don't let extra-curricular activities take over! [Not the person who disliked extra-curricular activities earlier.]

MS#3: Avoid clerical tasks. Work with the teacher as a co-designer of the curriculum. Work with kids without doing the task for them, and avoid unpleasant situations (example: fines).

MS#1: Expose children and youth to as much literature and media as possible. Develop *independent* users of the library media center. It is important for the media specialist to take a leadership position—because she sees all the children or youth and has access to the entire curriculum.

MS#2: Summed it all up with one word—"service."

The words of advice offered by these model media specialists to newcomers in the field also reveal their philosophies:

MS#5: Shove organization stuff into the background (get it done and then forget it)! You must be people-oriented, but you can't do that if you're not organized. Be a change agent! Go slowly, but do change—especially attitudes and relationships.

MS#4: Remember, most important is work with people—not bookkeeping. Even library skills are less important than people skills. The greatest obstacles you will face are adults—they are hardest to change. Evaluate often or you'll sit at the desk and never do the things libraries are about.

MS#3: Be an initiator! Establish communications with the teachers. Learn what's been done and learn the collection. You must know the collection in order to do curriculum work.

MS#2: Love kids! Love books, materials—information! Like school!

MS#1: Listen. Be enthusiastic. Be alert to opportunities. And enjoy!

The Portrait

With data from inventories, observations, and interviews, the profile of the model library media specialist becomes somewhat more distinct. Though the results of this research cannot be generalized to all successful library media specialists, there are patterns that emerge. The successful school library media specialist is one who:

- Has a positive self-concept

- May be shy/reserved but projects warmth

- Is bright, stable, enthusiastic, experimenting/exploring, trusting

- Is able to be self-sufficient

- Is confident of worth as an individual

- Enjoys people, work, variety/diversity

- Views change as a positive challenge

- Values communication

- Communicates effectively as an individual

- Is caring and especially attentive to others

- Is able and willing to clarify communication

- Is relatively self-disclosing

- Is uncomfortable with conflict

- Is confident of ability to deal with difficult situations in professional manner

- Is neither critical nor domineering

- Has no great need for achievement, power, or economic advantage

- Views self as leader in curriculum development

- Is willing to take the risks of being a leader

The portrait created is one that is interactive, dynamic, changing, radiating vitality, exuding of a confidence that says "Even though I may feel reserved or shy, I am capable of leadership because I believe people are important." This is the positive image—the self-concept—which school library media specialists need for themselves!

Recommendations

Though taken alone the results of this research are inconclusive, they may be used for further exploration in a variety of ways. For example:

1 The descriptors might be used as a self-evaluation checklist for persons interested in entering the field of school library media.

2 Library schools could utilize this positive image of library media specialists as vital, growing individuals interested in people and in change for recruiting efforts in the field.

3 Furthermore, since many library schools conduct entrance interviews, the checklist might be utilized by the interviewer—looking particularly for evidence of the candidate's ability to communicate effectively and be self-revealing, to demonstrate warmth, enthusiasm, attentiveness, a positive attitude, ability to clarify goals, and to be open to variety and change.

4 Administering the 16 PF (a relatively inexpensive tool that has been validated in a wide variety of settings) as a part of the introductory coursework that explores self and values in library schools would provide information valuable not only for counseling individual students, but also for sharpening the profile of persons interested in entering the field of library media.

5 Likewise, the Bienvenu Interpersonal Communications Inventory could be administered in coursework and utilized as a starting point for discussion and improvement of interpersonal communication (as suggested by the author of the inventory).

6 This study suggests that school library media specialists spend approximately three quarters of their time in oral communication —a strong mandate for schools of library and information management to have as a part of their required curriculum the teaching of interpersonal communication skills. (Such a statement assumes that even students who are relatively proficient in communicating can improve those abilities with practice.)

7 Changing one's communication style requires time and practice. Would the establishment of conversation/interaction groups to foster practice and change be effective in library schools?

8 Because the observational methodology utilized in this study was educational and beneficial to the observer/researchers, it could be used as a teaching tool. Students in library and information management might be asked: 1) to explore the categories of communications behavior; 2) to learn to recognize these behaviors in an actual situation and in themselves; 3) to observe model information professionals in the field; and 4) to collect data as was done in this study. Students would benefit in several ways: 1) by becoming aware of interpersonal communications styles; 2) by observing successful media and information professionals models at work; and 3) by experiencing a variety of information environments. The information profession would reap the benefit of having additional data about their members as well as (one hopes) more effective communicators at the entry levels and ultimately a more positive self-image!

9 At another level, principals and supervisors charged with hiring library media specialists might use the checklist for interviewing candidates. Certainly the checklist could not be used alone, but it could be a valuable guide for gathering information about the candidate.

10 On the job, and perhaps most beneficial to all, supervisors might utilize the structured observation technique to provide feedback to library media specialists concerning their communications patterns. In an accepting atmosphere, such information could be the basis for continued growth and enhancement of the positive self-concept of the library media specialist and the people with whom she works as well.

Whether the tools and methodology of this research are used or not, it is the positive picture of library media specialists as confident and effective communicators who enjoy people, variety, and change that we must retain and project. Most important, it is the way we must view ourselves.

Notes

1 Sandra M. Black, "Personality—Librarians as Communicators." *Canadian Library Journal* (April 1981):105–111.

2 Ibid., p. 67.

3 Edmund J. Amidon and Ned A. Flanders, *The Role of the Teacher in the Classroom: A Manual for Understanding and Improving Teachers' Classroom Behavior* (Minneapolis: Paul S. Amidon & Associates, 1963).

4 Alice I. Bryan, *The Public Librarian: A Report of Public Library Inquiry* (New York: Columbia University Press, 1952).

5 Robert R. Douglass, *The Personality of the Librarian* (Chicago: University of Chicago Press, 1957).

6 Black, p. 66.

7 Perry D. Morrison, *The Career of the Academic Librarian* (Berkeley: University of California, 1961).

8 Anne McMahon, *The Personality of the Librarian: Prevalent Social Values and Attitudes Toward the Profession* (Adelaide: Libraries Board of South Australia, 1967).

9 Howard Clayton, *An Investigation of Personality Characteristics Among Library School Students at One Midwestern University* (Washington, D.C.: United States Department of Health Education and Welfare, 1968).

10 David Sladen, "The Personality of the Librarian: An Investigation," *Library Association Record* (July 1972):118–19.

11 Robert Presthus, *Technological Change and Occupational Response: a Study of Librarians* (Toronto: York University Department of Political Science, 1970).

12 Kenneth Plate, *Management Personnel in Libraries: A Theoretical Model for Analysis* (Rockaway, NJ: American Faculty Press, 1970).

13 Presthus, p. 65.

14 Black, p. 67.

15 Richard Eggleton and Judith O'Dell, "Selecting Library Managers," *Drexel Library Quarterly* 17 (Summer 1981):1–13.

16 Ibid., p. 10.

17 Kenneth H. Plate and Jacob P. Siegel, "Career Patterns of Ontario Librarians," *Canadian Library Journal* (June 1979):143–48.

18 Black, p. 69.

19 Richard B. Eggleton, *Achievement Motivation Theory as It Relates to Professional Personnel at College and University Libraries* (Philadelphia: Drexel University, 1978).

20 Florence DeHart, *Interpersonal Relations in Libraries: A Seminar Experiment*, U.S., Educational Resources Information Center, ERIC Document ED 115 293, 1975.

21 Black, p. 68.

22 Sue E. Kenney and J. Kenney, "Personality Patterns of Public School Librarians and Teachers," *Journal of Experimental Education* (Spring 1982):152–53.

23 Jon R. Fortune and Andy Gibbons, "Emerging Personality Profiles of Colorado Library/Media Students," *Great Plains Libraries* (1981):18–23.

24 Jody Beckley Charter, "Case Study Profiles of Six Exemplary Public High School Library Media Programs" PhD dissertation, Florida State University, 1982.

25 Gordon W. Allport, Philip E. Vernon, and Gardner Lindzey, *Study of Values: A Scale for Measuring the Dominant Interests in Personality*, 3rd ed. (New York: Houghton Mifflin, 1970).

26 Millard J. Bienvenu, *Interpersonal Communication Inventory* (Natchitoches, LA: Northwestern State University, 1969).

Measures of Audiovisual Production Activities with Students

Grace Donoho

Studies indicate that reading interest peaks at the third and fourth grade. This means that teachers and library media specialists must expect to build extrinsic motivation into their reading programs if students beyond the fourth-grade level are to be drawn to print materials. Such has been the case at Old High Elementary School in Bentonville, Arkansas which serves only grades five and six plus three special education classes. A concerted effort over a period of years has been made to use the production of audiovisual media as a tool to help students make the transition from fiction to nonfiction and to help serve as a bridge for nonreaders to print materials.

The following case study has two purposes: first, to provide an in-depth picture of a library media program that uses local audiovisual production as a central focal point of service, and secondly, to provide a technique for the measurement of the impact of that service.

The concept of providing media literacy to each child as part of the library media program in the school is supported in the professional literature but is not widely applied. Concentration on library skills that are most often print-oriented and result in research reports and worksheet completion are more commonplace. Knowing that young people need highly motivating activities to keep them interested in the educational process, the library media specialist and the teachers at Old High have joined forces to make audiovisual production a means to achieve this end. The hypotheses have been that: 1) the introduction of media skills will result in more student interaction with print media; 2) media literacy and production skills will help students build self-esteem and confidence; and 3) media skills will be a tool to help students acquire curricular skills.

During a typical school year there are approximately 500 students enrolled at Old High Elementary School. The student body is divided into twenty-two classes, each of which has a scheduled fifty-minute class in the library media center (LMC). Nine of the classes are fifth grade, ten are sixth grade, two are unclassified special education, and one is for severely emotionally disturbed students.

The library media center is housed in a separate building and is open during the entire school day. Students may come at any time as long as they have a signed pass from their classroom teacher. A full-time aide assists the library media specialist with clerical work and supervision of the circulation desk as well as other assigned duties.

Due to spacious physical facilities, two classes can be accommodated with ease, in addition to small groups of students working on audiovisual productions in an area adjacent to the circulation desk.

A Typical Day in the Library Media Center

The following is a typical Friday schedule at Old High Library Media Center. There are five scheduled classes and two resource times. Resource times allow for special projects at a teacher's request. There are thirteen resource slots, each fifty minutes long, during any given week. At present, ten resource slots are being utilized.

First Period. Adventure Book Unit: Resource Period

The library media specialist team taught with a fifth-grade language arts teacher to develop a unit on adventure books. Students received a packet stating the unit objectives and assignments. As a final project, students wrote their own adventure story and prizes were awarded to the writers of the most adventuresome stories.

Second Period. Career Unit: Scheduled Sixth-Grade Class

The teacher of this class had met with the library media specialist during the summer and expressed concern about her students. This class was working below grade level and the students saw no reason for staying in school, much less doing their work. A career unit was planned to help. Students used reference tools to investigate their career choices and gave oral reports on their research. They searched through newspapers to assess the availability of

Measures of Audiovisual Production Activities with Students

their chosen career, possible wages, schooling requirements, and also typical living costs. A series of filmstrips was shown on possible ways to select a career (i.e., investigating hobbies and interests). Students then planned practice interviews using the video cassette recorder.

Third Period. Newbery Book Unit: Scheduled Sixth-Grade Class

Students were shown the filmstrip adaptation of *The Door in the Wall* by Marguerite de Angeli. This book tied in with the period in history being covered in their social studies class and also with Handicap Awareness Week.

Fourth Period. Lunch: Independent Work

When students have eaten, they may come to the LMC if they have a signed pass. They work on a variety of activities: doing research, creating media products, shelving books, putting up bulletin boards, checking out books, viewing filmstrips, or listening to cassettes.

Fifth Period. Media Production Unit: Scheduled Fifth-Grade Class

This class came twice a week to work on a slide/sound production titled "Special Libraries in the United States." Students indicated to the library media specialist the type of library they would like to learn about, i.e., military, motion picture, science, etc. The library media specialist went to a neighboring university library to locate addresses for those types of libraries. Then the students wrote letters to the library of their choice. While awaiting the arrival of materials, the students learned photography skills, storyboarding, graphics, and evaluated previously done student slide/sound productions.

Sixth Period. Almanac Unit: Scheduled Fifth-Grade Class

Through filmstrips and hands-on experience, students learned how to use the almanac. Small groups then worked to solve answers to mystery clues.

Seventh Period. Encyclopedia Unit/State Study: Scheduled Fifth-Grade Class

Students selected a state to research in the encyclopedia for social studies. They wrote to state capitals to obtain additional information. The finished reports included some form of appropriately used media.

A fifth-grade teacher teamed with the library media specialist to introduce students to mystery books. Each student received a packet explaining the unit goals and requirements for all written work. Generally, requirements called for some type of media such as posters, handmade filmstrips or transparencies.

A Sample Student Audiovisual Project in Depth

The emphasis on any audiovisual production project is to integrate media skills into the curriculum. This means that the curricular objective has top priority, while media skills are of secondary importance. However, since learning a production skill is highly motivating to students, the activity helps to achieve the primary objective. The following example will serve as a case in point.

During a recent school year, a fifth-grade social studies teacher and the library media specialist worked on a unit with a low-level ability group. Since fifth graders study United States history, the unit developed involved the study of twentieth-century presidents. The activity of the unit was to create a slide/sound program about a president. To gather information, students were to determine if a presidential library existed for their president and, if so, to write that library for information. While waiting for materials to arrive, the library media specialist taught the class how to operate a Pentax K-1000.

After introducing the unit, drawing names of presidential libraries to write to, and dividing into small groups, the class was told that the best-written letter from each group would be sent to the designated library. A show of hands revealed that no one, including the instructors, had ever written to a presidential library, and as the letters were begun, it became apparent that the students knew very little about writing a business letter. The language arts teachers reviewed this skill and work continued.

One group of students never received a reply from their library and so was assigned to do the title and credit posters. After brainstorming, they came up with all the necessary information and were provided with pencils, rulers, erasers and letters to trace.

As material from the libraries arrived, students worked with their group to determine what information to include in their section of

Measures of Audiovisual Production Activities with Students

the production. Each group was told they could use only five slides for their library. Storyboarding was explained and the chalkboard was used to demonstrate the process. The library media specialist used her life story as an example. When the groups began working on storyboarding, it was discovered that one group had decided that if five slides were good, twenty-five slides would be better!

After reflection, both the social studies teacher and the library media specialist felt that the students had learned a great deal about United States history, media literacy, and the unlimited patience of their instructors.

Other Typical Examples

Another social studies class studying the Civil War researched their favorite topic and created an original book. Much research time was spent prior to the actual construction of the cardboard book. Finished products were displayed in the LMC.

A sixth-grade social studies class, which was studying world cultures, came twice a week to work on a folktale/country study. The social studies instructor and the library media specialist selected countries the class would be studying and wrote the names down on slips of paper. Students drew for a country to determine who their partner would be. A packet was given each student detailing the objectives of the unit and requirements. The packet included all the assignments and paper required to complete the assignments.

During their scheduled library time, another class was involved in the study of folktales using Pied Piper's, "Folktales from Afar, Literature for Children, Series, 8." Each student team used the card catalog to locate folktales from their selected country. The team presented their favorite folktale using some form of media. Some planned to dress as an old-time storyteller and have their oral interpretation videotaped. Others used puppets, filmstrips, or transparencies. During one social studies period a week, this class came to the LMC and researched their country to locate information asked for in their packet. Specific data such as population, area, and hemisphere was being sought as well as information on the economy, people and education. Students decided to prepare food from their country and had an around-the-world tasting party. Once again students went to the card catalog to find cookbooks for recipes.

The severely emotionally-disturbed class learned about horn books used by colonial children. The high school shop teacher had his students cut out the basic shapes from scrap plywood. Students enjoyed the manual work of hand sanding and staining their horn books. Paper with the ABCs and a Bible verse was glued to the board. (One student insisted on printing on his board, "Truckers are neat people." No amount of talking would persuade him to change his mind, as he had decided to give his horn book to his father as a Christmas present.) Once while the class was busy sanding, the principal walked through the LMC making his rounds. He asked the students what they were doing. Their reply, "Making horny books!"

Measurements

Every library media center needs documentation as to the depth and breath of its program. This aids the library media specialist and the administration in evaluating the program and seeing that it has met its objectives. At Old High Elementary School, five measurements were used in documenting the audiovisual production aspect of the library media center program. These included: 1) use of a lesson plan book; 2) a longitudinal study of lesson plans; 3) a report to the principal; 4) a teacher survey; and 5) a student survey

Technique Number 1: Use of a Lesson Plan Book

One of the measures which can be used to document the library media center program is the lesson plan book. A little planning in the use of this book will provide information as to what goes on in the library media center, with whom, and at what depth.

Lesson plans are required by the principal at Old High Elementary School. This requirement extends to the library media specialist as well as the teachers. In designing the plans used for the library media center scheduling, color coding is done for the copy received by the principal.

In each date square of the planning page, the classroom teacher's name and library media center checkout number are written in black ink. Below that, in red ink, is the title of the unit of study being covered. Every nonscheduled class that comes to the library media center during resource time is recorded in red, including the teacher's name and the unit being covered.

This color coding alerts the principal to several things: first, the variety of units covered throughout the week in regularly scheduled classes, and second, the activities taking place during open or resource times. For example, during one week ten additional projects were occurring during resource times, each being a separate unit developed to support the curriculum.

Technique Number 2: A Longitudinal Study of Lesson Plans

It's one thing to look over lesson plans made for a week, but looking back over a long period of time helps the library media specialist and the principal discern the growth of the program, the breadth of the service, and the depth of the service.

The library media specialist at Old High compiled data from lesson plans covering the first four and one-half years that the school was in existence. Forty-three different classroom teachers taught at the school during those years. During this time frame, 74 percent of the teachers had students involved in media productions that were curriculum-related. These included handmade filmstrips for book reports, transparency sets depicting Civil War uniforms, videotapes of dental health week plays, a slide/sound production of unusual animals of the world, and doodle films as an art form, among others.

It was evident that 23 percent of the staff had students do cross-disciplinary audiovisual productions during that period of time. Examples of these included the art teacher and a language arts teacher teaming together on a slide/sound production. Students kept dream journals and then made cellophane slides to depict interesting entries in them.

The music teacher and a language arts teacher had students develop a slide presentation on the county in which the school is located. The language arts teacher assisted in helping the students write lyrics for an original song composed by the music teacher. The library media specialist taught a photography unit and the class took a field trip through the county to photograph important sights.

Technique Number Three: Report to the Principal

Library media specialists need to recognize that a principal who is an instructional leader in the school needs to know what is happening in the library media center. Brief and pointed notes to the principal as instructional involvement occurs is one excellent way to communicate program thrusts. An example of such a note follows:

Dennis,

Gayle Keesee and I met today to plan some combined language arts/library activities for the afternoon classes next year. Here are our planned activities:

I. Second Nine Weeks—Media
I will be researching at the university library to locate names and addresses of *special* libraries in the United States. Mrs. Keesee will review letter-writing skills so each small group will be able to write a concise letter asking for information on "their library." I will then teach 35mm photography skills. The end result will be a slide/sound production on special libraries located throughout the United States.

II. Third Nine Weeks—The Study of Different Types of Literature
A. Mystery Book Unit
B. Biographies
Students will be required to read a book and then work through a series of worksheets that demand high-level thinking.

III. Fourth Nine Weeks—Creative Dramatics
Students will produce and direct a play. Speakers from local theater groups will serve as resource people. Students will learn set design, make-up techniques, vocal techniques, directing techniques, etc. The play will be presented to the student body and parents. It will also be videotaped for OHE archives.

Grace Donoho

Technique Number Four: Teacher Survey

Through a survey, the school library media specialist can elicit unbiased opinions about the library media center's programming and its effect on the total school curriculum.

There are 31 certified teachers at Old High Elementary School. Thirteen of these teachers plus the principal from the 1983/84

Measures of Audiovisual Production Activities with Students

school year were surveyed to determine the degree of awareness of the types of production that take place in the library media center and also to ascertain their opinion as to the effect audiovisual production has on student attitudes. Teachers omitted from the survey included the library media specialist, the migrant tutor and other special services personnel. The library media center aide was responsible for collecting the data. The results of the survey are as follows:

Teacher Survey

1. What types of audiovisual production do the students of this school do, which is promoted by the library media center?

a. transparencies	93%
b. handmade filmstrips	93%
c. posters using the opaque projector	100%
d. slide/sound productions	57%
e. video tapes	79%
f. color lift slides	21%

2. Does audiovisual production contribute to what students learn in curricular areas such as language arts, social studies, science and reading?

Yes   100%

Comments:

"Yes, in order to make an audiovisual production they must do some research, and learning will take place in the process."

"Definitely—Good enrichment promotes other learning styles."

"Yes! In the past I have used the library media center to enhance the study and appreciation of different types of literature. Presently the library media center and my afternoon language arts class are engaged in a project wherein we will make a slide presentation on different and unusual types of libraries."

"I feel audiovisual production, in conjunction with my language arts classes, contributes a great deal to a child's enjoyment and understanding of a book. For my lower-ability children, it is an outlet (other than the stock book report) that they can succeed in, be proud of, and often excel in. In my higher-ability group, it is an opportunity for them to stretch their imagination and creativity as well as challenge them (which is often hard to do)."

3. Have you noticed any positive or negative effects on student attitudes when they are involved in media production?

	Positive	Negative
a. self-concept	93%	7%

"Yes, especially in lower-
ability groups."
"Develops an 'I can' attitude."
"They feel confident through
mechanical manipulation."

	Positive	Negative
b. motivation	93%	7%

"Yes, especially in lower groups."
"It's fun and different."
"Far more interested in the topic."

	Positive	Negative
c. creativity	93%	7%

"Extremely so—sixth graders seem
to want to exert their ideas and
personalities and *will* do it
in a creative way in media,
whereas they feel bound by peer
pressure in a peer group."
"The activity is creative."
"Yes, especially in higher
ability groups."

	Positive	Negative
d. attitude	93%	7%

"Pride! Self-achievement."
"Yes, children find books
can be fun."

e. Other?
"Contributes to overall learning."

Overall comment:

"This method of instruction is highly motivational. The students must give much thought to the visual. They have a better attitude in that *they* are producing something which they are responsible for. More self-evaluation of their product takes place also."

4. Do students actually learn enough media skills that they can create media or operate audiovisual equipment without close supervision?

Yes—50%

"Many of my students know more about running projectors, computers, and recorders than I do and often times I let them run the machines. They love to learn to use the equipment."

Most—21%

"Some need supervision, but if the teacher stimulates the activity, students work well with minimum supervision."

Don't know—14%
No—14%

"They need more instruction, especially in creating filmstrips, slides, using the VCR and in general planning skills."

5. Do students use print materials for research as a result of media production requirements? If yes, are there any discernible benefits?

Yes—71%

"In my class they were required to research a topic before putting it into an audiovisual report. The transition between written and oral report was interesting. In some cases it showed me their weak points in comprehension; in others, the students learned that to be effective meant to condense, simplify and/or delete as well as organize materials."

"Yes, they learn where to look for information and how to locate it quickly on their own with little or no adult supervision. This will be of great benefit to them in the future."

"The library media center is very active in teaching research methods. The teachers of the school do take advantage of the quality of the library media center and its programs and make it the hub of learning."

"Students use research skills in finding materials from encyclopedias, dictionaries, library books (card catalog) on their own and from other sources with guidance from a teacher or the librarian. It makes using the basic skills more fun when working on a special media project."

Don't know   29%

"I don't know. The students working on productions in art usually begin with a written story or print materials as motivators."

Measures of Audiovisual Production Activities with Students

Technique Number Five: Student Survey

Often the same patrons frequently use the library media center. So, from time to time it is best to survey students to get a broader view as to what they perceive is going on in the library media center and how it affects them.

A student survey was conducted to assess the following: the types of audiovisual materials produced in the library media center; the two favorite things the students do when at the library media center; how many have helped make media things in the library media center; whether they come in extra times to work on productions; and if they use print to help obtain information for the creation of media.

A sampling of 260 students from a total population of 495 was taken. One hundred thirty students from the fifth grade and 130 students from sixth grade participated in the survey. The results follow.

Student Survey

1. Which of the following types of audiovisual products do students work with in the library media center?

	5th	6th
a. transparencies	67%	95%
b. handmade filmstrips	53%	90%
c. posters using the opaque projector	87%	92%
d. slide/sound productions	70%	71%
e. video tapes	54%	83%
f. color lift slides	25%	53%
g. other	31%	21%

2. Of the following, which are your two favorite things to do when you come to the library media center?

	5th	6th
a. look at books and read	22%	17%
b. check out books	13%	12%
c. look at filmstrips	14%	7%
d. use the opaque projector	12%	10%
e. make filmstrips, transparencies, doodle films, color lift slides	11%	15%

		5th	6th
f.	work with the video equipment	10%	24%
g.	do photography with the 35mm camera	18%	15%

3. Have you helped make media things in the library media center?

	5th	6th
Yes	70%	90%
No	30%	10%

If no, do not answer questions 4 and 5.

4. Do you ever use extra time, such as during recess, to work on media in the library media center?

	5th	6th
Yes	47%	83%
No	23%	7%

5. When you create media do you have to use books, encyclopedia, magazines, and newspapers to get information to help you?

	5th	6th
Yes	57%	85%
No	13%	5%

The student survey reflects the impact of audiovisual production on the students. As the student becomes more involved in production, the more frequently he or she comes to the library media center.

While fifth and sixth graders' reading interest is on the downward slope, student audiovisual production stimulates them to go from pleasure reading to informational reading—from fiction to nonfiction.

A variety of audiovisual production skills are taught at the library media center, as indicated by the survey. Students enjoy being introduced to these skills and enjoy having the freedom to create an original production.

Conclusion

Student audiovisual production and media skills are an essential component of the library media program at Old High Elementary

School. As such, the students not only become familiar with production techniques but are drawn into the world of print. This bridge to the print world has been very effective as the data from various evaluative instruments show.

From this case study, three recommendations might be offered to other library media specialists in the field. First, involving students in audiovisual production as a central part of a total library media program has a great deal of potential and merit. Library media specialists who do not take advantage of the motivational assets of audiovisual production should reassess their program priorities.

Second, it is possible through the use of lesson plans, longitudinal studies, reports to principals, teacher surveys, and student surveys to provide needed documentation of the value and worth of a library media program.

Third, audiovisual production in and of itself requires that the student interact with the world of print. To be able to create an audiovisual product, accurate information must be obtained, digested, and rewritten as the basis of a script. In the minds of teachers, this type of activity clearly has an impact on learning in addition to being a highly motivating activity. Many teachers comment on the improvement of the students' self-concepts as they see their product come into existence and have it shown to others.

Media Utilization in the Classroom

Melvin McKinney Bowie

The case for the use of media in the classroom is a convincing one.[1] Research tells us that media have the capacity to involve students in their own learning, to capture students' attention, to extend their minds, to bring the outside world into the classroom, to evoke response, and to broaden and enhance the overall school experiences of young people. More specific, media are effective in teaching facts and concepts, sharpening inquiry and discovery skills, teaching psychomotor skills, changing attitudes, and in facilitating student motivation for learning. Research also reminds us that media are often more time-saving and less expensive than conventional teaching and are generally easy to use.

The literature also provides a number of research-tested guidelines to help teachers in the effective use of instructional media in the classroom. These guidelines cover procedures to be employed by the teacher prior to, during, and after a mediated lesson. Adherence to these procedures could mean the difference between a highly productive lesson and an unproductive one.

This article will first discuss the research literature pertaining to media utilization guidelines. The discussion will be confined basically to experimental studies conducted over the last thirty-five years. Research findings will be reported as general conclusions with little attention to detailed descriptions of individual experiments.

The second part of this article will then describe the results of a recent study of the current media utilization practices in elementary and secondary school classrooms. The study was conducted in early 1985 and was a poll of the perceptions of teachers concerning twenty-two statements taken from the research literature.

The final part of the article will suggest a method for evaluating media utilization practices in an individual school. Two proposed instruments containing cited practices from the research are included as workable tools for collecting data needed to improve the methods that teachers use in teaching with media.*

Introductions

It is widely recommended that teachers introduce all media presentations to the class.[2] Introductions increase the amount of learning from filmed material because they direct the students in observing pertinent points prior to viewing. Leestma has stated, "If no directions for observations are given to the viewers, each individual will interpret the scenes in his own way."[3] Kuhns and Stanley point out that instructional media (films) often lack interpretation or a fixed point of view, therefore the introduction serves as a mechanism to develop expectancy and readiness on the part of the students to receive a particular stimulus. The introduction also helps the students to identify the stimulus in question and to help them in "properly structuring the field."[4] Arwady states that introductions to filmed material are important because, "in delivering an oral introduction, the teacher becomes part of the film experience."[5]

In directing student observations prior to a media showing, certain techniques are recommended.[6] These include the following:

1 Previewing the media

2 Giving advance assignments that are related to the content of the presentation

3 Posing questions that the presentation will answer

4 Briefly outlining the content of the presentation and discussing this outline

5 Briefly discussing the relationship of the presentation to previous lessons

6 Explaining unusual techniques used in the media

A study with seventh graders revealed that providing an introduction which included the technical vocabulary used in a film, a general description of the film's content along with a statement of

---

* This article was prepared with the assistance of Kenneth Baumgarner and Judy Mackey, graduate students at the University of Arkansas.

purpose, and questions about the concepts to be presented in the film significantly increased the test scores of those students receiving the introduction.[7] In another study with high school students, Arwady found that a substantive oral introduction to a film increased student learning at all ability levels. A substantive introduction was defined as "a general synopsis of film content, which is delivered in an attempt to familiarize the audience with the entire film on a broad and inclusive basis."[8]

Student Participation and Discussion

Research findings suggest that teachers should work to increase the level of learner participation through discussion of a mediated presentation in order to improve the effectiveness of the lesson.[9-17] Providing students with opportunities to participate in class discussions after film or television viewings significantly increased learning. At least one study emphasized the importance of an active response to television programs to increase their effectiveness.[18] Quinney, also, reported research findings that support the use of discussion to improve the effectiveness of film viewing: "The techniques of using introductory questions and holding discussion after viewing thus induced the students to become active participants in the learning experience rather than passive bystanders. Introduction and discussion are therefore of crucial importance."[19]

While most of the studies on the value of discussions in mediated lessons analyzed results when such discussions were held after the viewing exercises, there is some evidence to support the practice of stopping the presentation at strategic points to hold such discussions.[20] In a study with seventh-grade girls, gains in learning were significant when a film presentation was interrupted for purposeful discussion. The time of discussion appears to be unimportant so long as students are allowed opportunities for the exchange of ideas and dialogue about the material being presented. Students have even been known to complain when they were denied such opportunities.[21,22]

Kuhns and Stanley have provided teachers with valuable guidelines for leading discussions after a film showing.[23] In order for the discussions to aid students in mastering the material, the teacher should 1) listen to what each person in the class has to say, 2) relate each comment to the previous speakers, and 3) emphasize the way or ways in which the camera communicates the message.

The idea is to provide clarification and amplification of the information presented in the media and to provide students with a common reference point concerning the presentation.

The Use of Questions

Some studies have attempted to determine the effectiveness of asking questions about the content of a media presentation. Quinney searched the film literature and found evidence that the use of questions prior to and immediately after showing the film, along with providing answers to the questions, significantly influenced learning.[24] This technique was found to be more effective than asking no questions, asking questions only before viewing, or asking questions only after viewing. Quinney believes that the most important questions were those that helped the student to view the information critically.

Richard Hirsch provides other evidence which suggests that repeating the questions and providing the answers during a discussion result in increased learning.[25] His particular study found that one of the important elements in learning from film is to provide learners with correct feedback to questions that have been posed by the film during the discussion. Math and science students in Cincinnati who were taught via television complained about the lack of questions during the presentations. They felt that the use of questions would have facilitated understanding and appreciation of the material.[26]

Repeated Showings

Earlier summaries of the research literature on media utilization have concluded that showing the material more than once increases the amount of information learned by students.[27,28,29,30] Allen discussed several studies that found that though most learning took place during the initial showing of a film, a second showing increased learning substantially. One study found that this increase was at least 32 percent. A third showing of the film failed to add significantly to the amount of material learned, and a fourth showing actually decreased learning.[31] Hoban and van Ormer also reviewed the literature and concluded that most of the

Media Utilization in the Classroom

learning occurred after the second showing of a film, but that additional showings were a waste of time.[32] Most teachers, however, rarely have the teaching time to repeat a presentation; therefore, repeating only those parts that were not clearly understood might be a useful compromise.[33]

Even reducing the rate of presentation does not appear to increase learning beyond the second showing of a film.[34] Navy trainees found that a slow rate of film development produced the best learning but did not increase learning beyond the second showing. A fast version of the film ran for 3 minutes, while the slow version was presented in 4.5 minutes. Further research reported that a second showing of a televised lesson was effective when no further instruction was given by the teacher, but was not effective when additional instruction was provided.[35] Research in Australia with high school students found a high correlation between the amount of learning and repeated film showings.[36] Gropper and Lumsdaine found that repeating what was poorly learned in a television program was helpful to junior high school science students in Pittsburgh.[37] Hirsch concluded from a study with military trainees that repeating the showing of a film reduced forgetting and made possible new learning.[38]

Follow-Up Activities and Feedback

Providing students with answers to questions about the content of an audiovisual presentation has been found to significantly increase the amount of material learned.[39,40,41,42,43] The importance of feedback in learning was demonstrated when researchers found that when students with high IQs were denied feedback to questions about televised lessons in geometry and reading, their test scores dropped and became significantly lower than those of students of lesser ability.[44] Knowledge of correct responses to test questions or discussion questions appears to serve as an important factor in motivating students to learn from media.

The above researchers also found that follow-up activities to media presentations reinforced learning and significantly reduced forgetting. Review exercises, workbook assignments, outside reading assignments, laboratory work, and other projects following a media presentation are useful in reinforcing learning.[45] Testing students about the content of the presentation not only provides the teacher with data concerning the effectiveness of the media, but serves to reinforce facts and concepts presented in the material. Testing also encourages students to respond actively to the presentation. Stein conducted research which concluded that pre-film testing was also an effective way to aid learning.[46]

Taking Notes

The value of taking notes during an audiovisual presentation is questionable. Redemsky reported that students found taking notes while viewing a film of little value.[47] Students, therefore, tended not to take notes. Note taking during a planned break in a film showing has been found to be beneficial only to very bright students.[48] Other research has suggested that note taking during a film showing distracts attention from the film and interferes with learning.[49] Earlier A-V studies concluded that the rapid rate of development of the visual and narrative elements in a film made note taking ineffective.[50]

Physical Environment for Viewing

Consideration of the physical environment in which instructional media are presented has been the subject of a number of studies. Levels of room illumination, seating arrangements, viewing angles, room size, and noise levels in the room have all been investigated. There is general agreement in the literature that low levels of room illumination are more desirable than a completely darkened room when viewing films.[51,52] Denno studied the desirable levels of light falling on the screen during projections of black and white and color films. Using a panel of teachers as judges, the study found that .15 foot candles of light on the screen was most desirable during projection. Illumination beyond that level tended to distort the images on the screen. An earlier recommendation had suggested that light levels on the screen should not exceed .10 foot candles.[53] Levels of room illumination do not appear to be crucial in film viewing unless viewers are seated more than 12 screen widths from the screen.[54] Navy trainees learned more from a film shown in a dark room when they were seated great distances from the screen.

Seating arrangements and viewing angles have been found to have little influence on the amount of information learned by viewers. "Most likely instructional procedures, which are relatively independent of room illumination, viewing angle and distance from

Media Utilization in the Classroom

the screen, are the most important factors of audience response, as far as factual learning is concerned."[55] It has also been found that students learn equally as well when viewing media in a large auditorium as when watching the same presentations in a small classroom.[56]

Noise levels in the viewing room can be an important consideration when teaching with media.[57] When six groups of students viewed electricity concepts on film or television, the groups with noisy film projectors learned significantly less than did students who watched TV monitors or who used a quiet film projector. Findings from this study suggest that teachers should attempt to keep noise levels at a minimum in the viewing area.

Summary of Utilization Guidelines

Research has provided the classroom teacher with tested guidelines for effective utilization of media in a teaching situation. Based on analyses of the literature by this writer and earlier writers, the following recommendations for the use of instructional media are made:

1 Preview all media before showing.

2 Formally prepare the students to receive the information to be presented. This should be done through a substantive overview of the content, pointing out important things that they should look for.

3 Allow the students the time and opportunity to discuss the presentation. This can be done by posing questions prior to or after the showing.

4 Always provide reinforcement to the presentation through follow-up activities and feedback to questions or other responses from students.

5 Repeat the showing of a presentation when possible, or at least repeat those parts that need clarification.

6 Remember that repeating a showing more than once does not aid learning.

7 Do not require note taking during viewing exercises.

8 Do not show media in a completely darkened room unless the aim is to create a given mood or unless the students are seated more than 12 screen widths from the screen. Otherwise, a dimly lighted room is recommended.

9 Keep noise levels in the viewing room at a minimum.

10 Do not become overly concerned about the viewing angle of the viewers or the size of the viewing area. These factors will have little influence on the amount of learning that takes place.

Current Teacher Use of Guidelines

In order to evaluate the level of teacher use of the above recommended guidelines, principals, library/media specialists, and other teachers in two southern states were asked to identify teachers who were regular users of instructional media in their classrooms. One hundred such teachers were identified. They were then asked to complete a 22-item checklist concerning their current practices in using four types of instructional media. These media were 16mm motion picture film, television/video, filmstrips, and slides.

Respondents were given four options in describing the frequency with which they adhered to the guidelines. These options were: *1* = never; *2* = sometimes; *3* = often; and *4* = always. In addition to describing their media utilization practices, responding teachers were asked to indicate the level of the school in which they worked and the number of years they had taught. It was reasoned that differences in utilization practices, if any, might be attributed to the age group with which the teacher worked or to the teacher's level of classroom experience.

Eighty-seven percent of the one hundred teachers returned usable checklists. Forty-nine percent of the respondents taught at the elementary school level, while the other fifty-one percent were secondary school teachers. Twenty-one percent of the teachers had less than five years of teaching experience. Thirty-six percent had taught five to ten years, and forty-three percent had taught more than ten years. These figures indicated a great deal of classroom experience among the responding teachers.

Filmstrips were used regularly by thirty-seven percent of the responding teachers. Twenty-eight percent reported that they used 16mm films, and twenty-three percent made use of television/video. Only twelve percent of the subjects used photographic slides in their teaching.

Table 1
Frequency Means for Utilization Guidelines
(n = 87)

		Level		Experience		
*PSG Items	All	Elem.	Sec.	0–4	5–10	10+
1 Provide overview	3.4	3.3	3.5	3.4	3.2	3.5
2 Prior questions	2.7	2.7	2.7	2.8	2.6	2.7
3 Provide outline	2.2	2.1	2.2	2.2	2.2	2.1
4 Give objectives	3.0	2.8	3.2	2.8	2.9	3.2
5 Direct observation	3.2	3.1	3.3	3.0	3.1	3.4
6 Preview media	3.0	2.5	3.4	2.5	3.2	3.0
**DSG Items						
7 Dim lighting	3.5	3.4	3.6	3.2	3.2	3.4
8 Interrupt showing	2.5	2.6	2.5	2.3	2.5	2.8
9 Require notes	1.9	1.6	2.1	1.5	1.9	2.0
***ASG Items						
10 Allow discussion	3.3	3.2	3.4	3.3	3.3	3.3
11 Repeat showing	1.7	1.6	1.8	1.4	1.8	1.8
12 Follow-up activity	2.5	2.4	2.6	2.4	2.6	1.8
13 Questions after	3.3	3.2	3.3	3.3	3.4	3.2
14 Test over content	2.4	2.2	2.6	2.8	2.5	2.2
20 Provide feedback	3.5	3.4	3.7	3.6	3.5	3.6
Supplementary Items						
15 Achieved objective	2.8	2.8	2.9	2.8	2.7	2.8
16 Students motivated	2.4	2.6	2.7	2.3	2.3	2.5
17 To introduce unit	2.4	2.3	2.5	2.2	2.6	2.4
18 To summarize unit	2.5	2.4	2.6	2.3	2.7	2.5
19 To enrich unit	2.9	2.9	3.0	2.9	3.0	2.9
21 Students enjoy	3.5	3.6	3.5	3.6	3.4	3.6
22 For entertainment	1.7	1.9	1.6	1.9	1.7	1.6

* Pre-showing guidelines.
** During-showing guidelines.
*** Post-showing guidelines.

SCALE: 1 = Never
2 = Sometimes
3 = Often
4 = Always

Findings

Responses to each item on the checklist were totaled and computed as averages. The average responses were then stratified by school level and years of teaching experience. Table 1 contains checklist item numbers, abbreviated statements of the items, overall averages for each item, and average responses of the five classification groups.

Analyses of the data revealed a general adherence to the media utilization guidelines in the literature. This conclusion was applicable for both elementary and secondary teachers, and for experienced and inexperienced teachers. While there was no single practice which teachers used "Always" or "Never," there were overall tendencies in the recommended directions.

Pre-Showing Items

Table 1 indicates that most teachers use recommended guidelines prior to showing media. All groups reported that they often (3.4) provide students with an overview of the presentation, often (3.0) provide students with the objectives of the showing, and often (3.2) tell students what to look and listen for during the show. The teachers tended to use questions prior to the showings and to provide students with outlines of the content to be presented less frequently. The frequency means for these two latter practices were 2.7 for posing questions prior to the showing, and 2.2 for distributing outlines. Comments from some of the respondents indicated that outlines were provided orally during introductions, therefore written outlines seemed unnecessary. They also thought that written outlines were too time consuming, and their distribution tended to distract the attention of students from the verbal introductions by the teacher.

Frequency means for the practice of previewing the media prior to using indicated some differences between elementary and secondary teachers and between experienced and inexperienced teachers. Elementary teachers reported that they only previewed A-V materials slightly more than sometimes (2.5), while secondary teachers previewed materials slightly more than often (3.4). Teachers who had worked less than five years previewed materials less frequently (2.5) than did those who had worked longer than five years (3.2 for five to ten years group, and 3.0 for more than ten years group). One teacher commented that the district library media specialist previewed all films and videotapes for the district center and distributed detailed descriptions of the materials. Therefore, individual teachers in that district did not need to preview these materials. Nonetheless, it generally appears that elementary school teachers are given less opportunity to become familiar with media prior to use than are secondary teachers. It also seems that the most experienced teachers realize the value of previewing more than do newer teachers. These speculations need to be investigated through further research.

During-the-Show Items

With regards to the three guidelines pertaining to practices to be followed while showing the media, the teachers in all groups were consistent in their responses. More often than not (3.5), they maintained dim lighting in the viewing room and almost never (1.9) required students to take notes during the show. The frequency with which they stopped the projector for discussion and other activities was slightly above the "sometimes" level, with 2.5 as the overall average for this practice. The levels of these practices were all tending toward the directions recommended in the literature.

Post-Showing Items

Six guidelines for practices to be used following the showing of instructional media were gleaned from the literature. Responses to these six items on the checklist revealed little deviation among the teachers in this sample. They often (3.3) allow for discussion, often (3.3) pose questions about the presentation, and very often (3.5) provide students with feedback to all discussion questions. Testing students on the content of a presentation was not a very popular practice. The same was true for assigning follow-up activities. The latter finding was disappointing in light of the stress placed on the effectiveness of follow-up activities in the literature. The teachers almost never repeated a media presentation. This finding was not surprising as there is often little class time left for a repetition of presentations. Also, most A-V materials, particularly films and video tapes, are scheduled only for short periods in a given school and must be returned soon after using to the circulating agency. Thus, teachers have difficulty in attempting to repeat a showing when it is needed.

Supplementary Items

The checklist also contained a number of supplementary statements pertaining to utilization practices and to possible presentation outcomes. Respondents were asked to indicate the frequency with which they engaged in these practices or the frequency with which they perceived that a given outcome occurred.

Overall responses to the item which asked respondents for the perceived frequency with which students achieved the objectives of the mediated lessons approached the "often" level (2.8). This pattern of perceptions was consistent across all groups. Without data from more frequent testing about the presentations, this finding would seem reasonable.

It was disappointing that students were motivated only "sometimes" (2.4) to search for further information or to read additional materials after presentations. One of the important attributes of the media is their capacity to serve as motivating factors in individual learning.[58] However, the frequency with which teachers in the study used follow-up activities (2.5) could account partially for the lack of student motivation to individually engage in additional learning activities.

When asked how frequently they used the four types of media to introduce a unit of instruction, to summarize a unit, or to enrich a unit, teacher responses averaged slightly above the "sometimes" level. The same levels of frequency for these three practices were indicated when responses were stratified by school level and years of experience. It would appear that teachers use media for a variety of reasons in their classrooms.

The study found that students frequently enjoyed media presentations. The average frequency response to this item was 3.5. One teacher commented that students tended to enjoy the presentations more when they were used to enrich a unit.

Teachers almost never presented media as a form of pure entertainment. One teacher argued that while "pure entertainment" generally meant "not related to subject matter," the use of media presentations that were not directly related to the subject were often of value to students. This teacher, therefore, reported the frequent use of media for this purpose.

Conclusions

The findings from this study suggest a high level of teacher awareness of the recommended guidelines for the effective use of instructional media. The overall means for frequency responses to checklist items indicated little deviation between elementary and secondary teachers and among the three experience groups. In all three categories of guidelines—pre-showing, during the show, and post-showing, teachers tended to adhere to recommended practices. It would be reasonable to assume that the teachers identified for this study were those who are highly competent and are among those who represent a highly select group that is working in today's classrooms. Research has found that teachers who frequently used instructional films were those teachers who 1) had training in A-V production, 2) had access to trained media center personnel, and 3) had the encouragement of the administration to use films in their teaching.[59]

Webb reported after a study in Minnesota that principals rated teachers who were high users of films as being generally well-informed about films and familiar with the content of the films; they helped students search for information after a film showing, and used many different kinds of A-V materials in the classroom. Principals also considered these teachers to be the most effective teachers on the staff.[60] In Indiana, Leader and Null found "teachers who believed that audiovisual materials were valuable in the instructional process and that they increased motivation for learning utilized more films."[61] Teachers in elementary schools in this study tended to preview media less frequently than did secondary teachers. The same difference was true between less experienced and more experienced teachers. Perhaps additional research could help to explain this difference. Surprisingly, the study found that teachers infrequently test students about the content of a presentation. It would seem that very little attention is being given to the actual attainment of the specific learning objectives that were set forth during the introductions.

Recommendations for Daily Practice

It is recommended that principals and district administrators become aware of and evaluate the current media utilization practices in their individual schools and school districts. A systematic program of evaluation should, *first,* encourage all teachers to use media in their classrooms and to use them in the most effective manner possible. It is not enough to sit back and know that only the exceptional teachers are using media. The less talented teachers must also be encouraged to take advantage of more effective instructional techniques. Media have been found to significantly increase the instructional effectiveness of good, as well as poor, teachers.[62] *Second,* summaries of research findings on media utilization should be compiled and distributed to all teachers. If teachers are to use the best methods in mediated lessons, efforts must be made to provide teachers with information about such methods. Finally, discussion sessions of the summaries should be held so that teachers can compare in an open forum the recommended guidelines with their actual use. For example, such forums could explore the problems that teachers have in repeating media presentations as is recommended in the literature. Solutions to problems encountered in scheduling the use of films and video programs could be sought so that teachers could have the opportunity to keep materials longer as the need arises. Such forums could also allow teachers the opportunity to discuss the pros and cons of requiring students to take notes while viewing media programs. The literature suggests that if note taking is required it should be done during a break in the presentation when the projector is turned off. Some teachers feel, however, that note taking while viewing forces all students to pay close attention to the information being presented. Another area which could be explored during such discussions among teachers is that of testing students over the materials presented by the media. It could be that teachers do not feel that such tests are needed or that they are too time consuming. Whatever the reasons, some method of assessing the teaching effectiveness of the media should be identified and included as a regular part of a mediated lesson.

Evaluation Technique 1

Some assessment of media utilization can be accomplished through the use of a questionnaire or checklist, such as the one used in this study. The actual format of the questionnaire matters little so long as it provides the needed information on which to base sound conclusions about proper media utilization. A sample of the questionnaire used in this study is provided in appendix 1. The questionnaire is simple to use and can be easily modified to fit individual school situations. Information derived from use of the questionnaire can serve as a starting point for decision making in improving the effectiveness of media use in a given school.

Evaluation Technique 2

One of the important problems, however, with questionnaires

Media Utilization in the Classroom

used as data collection instruments in evaluation is that they provide only self-reports from the teachers. Therefore, some follow-up to the self-reports would be helpful. This follow-up could be observer ratings of teacher practices, which would provide an additional and a more objective assessment of such practices in a given classroom. Principals should consider the advantages of using an unbiased method such as outside observer ratings.

Observer forms could contain statements similar to those used in our checklist. (See appendix 2.) Observers using the form could simply indicate by checking whether a given behavior by the teacher was observed or not during a lesson in which media were used. The form should also contain the teacher's name, the grade level and subject of the lesson, and the type of media used.

Once the data from the observers' rating forms have been analyzed, it is then possible to plan inservice sessions to those teachers who appear to be in need of further training in implementing the guidelines. It could be found that several teachers are having problems with a single practice. The underlying causes of this problem should be sought and corrected through general inservice sessions.

Library media personnel in individual schools and at the district level could be utilized in assessing the media utilization practices in individual schools. These persons are generally familiar with the research literature and are most often aware of the attributes and capabilities of instructional materials. They are also knowledgeable about the media supply and demand conditions in the school and are sensitive to the problems that teachers face in acquiring materials for a given teaching situation. Media specialists, along with other teachers who have also been informed about and trained in the proper use of media, could serve as objective observers of utilization practices in the school. They are also the persons who could help in distributing findings from the evaluation procedures and in conducting the needed inservice training in the school.

Working together, principals, library media specialists, and teachers can evaluate and improve the instructional effectiveness of media in the classroom. Increased student learning would then be a natural outcome of such cooperative efforts.

Notes

1 *Encyclopedia of Educational Research,* Chester Harris 3rd ed., s.v. "Audio-Visual Communication," by W. H. Allen; *Handbook of Research on Teaching,* N. Gage 1963 ed., s.v. "Instruments and Media of Instruction," by A. A. Lumsdaine; G. Torkelson, "What Research Says to the Teacher: Educational Media." NEA, 1968; *Encyclopedia of Educational Research,* R. L. Ebel 1969 ed., s.v. "Educational Communications Media," by Loran Twyford; Sidney Tickton ed., *To Improve Learning,* Vol. I (New York: Bowker, 1970); and *Encyclopedia of Educational Research,* Harold Mitzel 5th ed., s.v. "Media Use in Education," by Warren Seibert and Eldon Ullmer.

2 Robert Leestma, "Directed Observation in Film Utilization," *Audio-Visual Communication Review* 2 (1954):103–108; Commonwealth Office of Education, "The Effective Use of Sound Films," *Audio-Visual Communication Review* 2 (1954):78–79; Francis Murphy, "The Relative Effectiveness of Filmed Introductions to a General Science Motion Picture," *Dissertation Abstracts* 22 (1961):3121–3122; William Kuhns and Robert Stanley, *Exploring the Film* (Fairfield, NJ: CEBCO Standard Pub., 1968); Twyford; Valerie Quinney, "Using Films in College Social Science Classes," *Improving College and University Teaching* 25 (1977):18–21; and Joseph Arwady, "The Oral Introduction to the Instructional Film: A Closer Look," *Educational Technology* 20 (1980):18–22.

3 Leestma, p. 104.

4 Ibid., p. 106.

5 Arwady, p. 19.

6 Leestma, p. 106.

7 Murphy.

8 Arwady, p. 20.

9 Commonwealth Office of Education.

10 Merwin Himmler, "An Analysis and Evaluation of a Television Demonstration of the Teaching of Fifth-Grade Reading, Arithmetic and French," *Dissertation Abstracts* 17 (1957):2467.

11 Louis Redemsky, "Student Evaluation of Films Used in College Social Studies," *Audio-Visual Communication Review* 7 (1959):3–13.

12 Allen.

13 Philip Minter et al., "Does Presentation Method Influence Film Learning?" *Audio-Visual Communication Review* 9 (1961):195–200.

14 George Gropper and A. A. Lumsdaine, "An Experimental Evaluation of the Contribution of Sequencing, Pretesting, and Active Student Responses to the Effectiveness of Programmed TV Instruction," *Audio-Visual Communication Review* 9 (1961):A-51–52.

15 Norma Walton, "A Pilot Study of Student Attitudes in a Closed-Circuit Television Course by Use of Stimulated Recall," *Dissertation Abstracts* 24 (1963):1082.

16 US, Department of HEW, Office of Education, *Research in Instructional Television and Film* (Washington, DC: Government Printing Office, 1967), (ERIC Document ED 015 673).

17 US, Department of HEW, Office of Education, "Review of Trends in Research on Instructional Television and Film," in *Research in Instructional Television and Film* (Washington, DC: Government Printing Office, 1967), (ERIC Document ED 015 673).

18 Gropper and Lumsdaine.

19 Quinney, p. 18.

20 Minter, et al.

21 Richard Evans, "An Examination of Students' Attitudes toward Television as a Medium of Instruction in a Psychology Course," *Journal of Applied Psychology* 40 (1956):32–34.

22 Reid and MacLennan.

23 Kuhns and Stanley.

24 Quinney.

25 Richard Hirsch. *The Effects of Knowledge of Test Results on Learning of Meaningful Material,* 1952. (ERIC Document ED 002 435).

26 Reid and MacLennan.

27 Allen.

28 Twyford.

29 Charles Hoban and Edward van Ormer, *Instructional Film Research, 1918–1950.* (New York: Arno Press, 1970).

30 Quinney.

31 Allen.

32 Hoban and van Ormer, pp. 8–43.

33 Quinney.

34 *The Effects and Interaction of Rate of Development, Repetition, Partic-ipation, and Room Illumination on Learning from a Rear Projected Film,* Philip Ash and Nathan Jaspen, SDC 269-7-39. Instructional Film Research Reports. US Naval Special Devices Center, 1953.

35 John Hayman and James Johnson, "Exact vs. Varied Repetition in Ed-ucational Television," *Audio-Visual Communication Review* 11 (1963):96–103.

36 Commonwealth Office of Education.

37 Gropper and Lumsdaine.

38 Hirsch.

39 Ibid.

40 Commonwealth Office of Education.

41 Francis Almstead and Raymond Graf. "Talkback: The Missing Ingre-dient." *Audio-Visual Instruction* 5 (1960):110–112.

42 Greenhill.

43 Reid and MacLennan.

44 Almstead and Graf.

45 Greenhill.

46 *The Effect of Pre-Film Test on Learning from an Educational Motion Picture.* J. J. Stein. SDC 269-7-35. Instructional Film Research Reports. US Naval Special Devices Center, 1952.

47 Redemsky.

48 Minter, et al.

49 Quinney.

50 Allen, p. 126.

51 Raymond Denno, "Classroom Screen Darkness Levels for Educational Film Projection," *Audio-Visual Communication Review* 6 (1958):5–22.

52 Allen, p. 126.

53 Ibid.

54 Ash and Jaspen.

55 Hoban and van Ormer.

56 Allen, p. 126.

57 J. F. McGrane and Morton Baron, "A Comparison of Learning Resulting from Motion Picture Projector and Closed Circuit Television Presentations," *Society of Motion Picture and Television Engineers Journal* 68 (1959):824–27.

58 Mark May and Nelle Lee Jenkinson, "Developing Interest in Reading with Film," *Audio-Visual Communication Review* 1 (1953):159–66.

59 Allen.

60 Harry Webb, "An Investigation of Teacher Characteristics and Educational Film Utilization in Three Minnesota Urban School Systems," *Dissertation Abstracts* 23 (1962):554–55.

61 Harry Leader and Eldon Null, "What Kind of Teachers Use Instructional Films?" *Audio-Visual Instruction* 19 (1974):42–46.

62 Wesley Meirhenry, *The Nebraska Program of Educational Enrichment through the Use of Motion Pictures.* (University of Nebraska, 1951).

Appendix 1: Media Effectiveness Evaluation

The purpose of this checklist is 1) to determine the levels of teacher awareness of guidelines for the proper utilization of instructional media and 2) to determine the extent to which these guidelines are currently being used in the classroom.

Please check or fill in the blank:

I teach ____Primary ____Intermediate ____Jr. High ____Sr. High.

I have taught _____years.

Think back over the past few months and identify those units of instruction in which you used one or more of the following types of media: (Check the applicable ones.)

____Motion picture film ____TV/Video ____Filmstrip
____Slides

Now, please circle the numerical option on the scale which best describes your practices in using these media with your class.

1 = Never   2 = Sometimes   3 = Often   4 = Always

1. I prepare the students for the presentation
   by giving them an overview of what to
   expect.   1   2   3   4

Media Utilization in the Classroom

124

2. I pose questions prior to the showing that
   will be answered during the presentation. 1 2 3 4
3. I provide the students with an outline or
   a summary of the content presented in
   the media. 1 2 3 4
4. I give the students the objectives of the
   presentation. 1 2 3 4
5. I tell the students what to look or listen
   for in the presentation. 1 2 3 4
6. I preview the media before using them
   with my class. 1 2 3 4
7. I show media in a dimly lighted room. 1 2 3 4
8. I stop the projector at strategic points to
   allow for questions and discussion. 1 2 3 4
9. I require students to take notes while
   viewing the presentation. 1 2 3 4
10. I allow the students time to discuss the
    material presented. 1 2 3 4
11. I show the presentation a second time for
    reinforcement or to clarify points that
    were not well understood. 1 2 3 4
12. I assign follow-up activities after the
    media presentation. 1 2 3 4
13. I pose questions after the presentation to
    spark discussion. 1 2 3 4
14. I test students on the content of the
    presentation. 1 2 3 4
15. Most of my students achieve the learning
    objectives of the presentation. 1 2 3 4
16. My students express interest in reading or
    finding more information about the
    subject matter of the presentation. 1 2 3 4
17. I use media to introduce an instructional
    unit. 1 2 3 4
18. I use media to summarize an instructional
    unit. 1 2 3 4
19. I use media to enrich an instructional unit. 1 2 3 4
20. I give students the correct answers to any
    questions about the presentation. 1 2 3 4
21. My students seem to enjoy media
    presentations. 1 2 3 4
22. I use media with my students purely for
    entertainment. 1 2 3 4

Appendix 2: Example Rating Form for Observing Media Utilization

Teacher's Name_____ **Date**_____
Grade_____ **Subject**_____ **Media Used**_____

Utilization Practice	Observed	Not Observed
Provided an overview		
Posed questions prior to show		
Provided written outline		
Gave the objectives		
Directed observations		
Dimmed the lighting		
Interrupted the show		
Required note taking		
Allowed for discussion		
Repeated the show		
Assigned follow-up activity		
Posed questions after show		
Provided feedback		
Tested on content		
Students enjoyed the show		
Students were motivated to seek additional information		

Observer's Name_____

Periodicals on Microfiche

Thomas H. Olsen

Background

Media specialists in the Boise Public School District often admitted to their supervisor that they felt uneasy about the quality of research service offered to students. The specialists generally felt that through accessing the book collections students could do an adequate job of finding needed research materials. However, when students were expected to access current sources of information, the whole research process took on an aura of frustration. Media specialists complained that after all their hard work in encouraging students to use indexing tools, they were often embarrassed when the needed magazine articles were not available even though the "holdings file" indicated that the magazine was in the school collection. Media specialists had become quite adept at offering logical explanations for the lack of service: "That particular issue was not received from the publisher." Or "We received that issue, but it was stolen the day after it arrived." Or "Here is the issue you requested; unfortunately, the article you wanted has been torn from the magazine." The students were not impressed.

Discussions between the district library supervisor and the building media specialists often centered on the "magazine problem." Though none of the specialists had an abundance of time to devote to new duties, three media specialists enthusiastically endorsed the idea of experimenting with the magazine problem in hopes of finding a suitable solution. The media specialists were particularly interested in experimenting with microfilm or microfiche magazine collections; the library supervisor was particularly interested in tracking student requests for magazines to determine which requests were filled and which were not. Media specialists and supervisor, alike, were interested in documenting the factors that led to a failed magazine search. Further discussions led the specialists and supervisor to believe that one research design could envelope all of the major concerns. One question remained, however: How could the project be funded?

Diverting funds from already meager materials and equipment accounts was out of the question. Likewise, transferring district funds from other departments to the media services department held little promise. The funding dilemma was answered through Title IV of the Elementary and Secondary Education Act. Part C of the act was to fund "Educational Innovation and Support." The purpose of the research project was to supply microfiche equipment and software to targeted junior high and senior high schools and then to measure the use of the total magazine collection, including hardcopy and microformats. The grant proposal was funded by the Idaho State Department of Education and covered the 1978, 1979 and 1980 school years. Though the Boise Public School District serves approximately 21,000 students in forty different buildings, only three of the district schools were targeted.

Formal Operations

Once the grant had been approved, a microfiche reader/printer, several microfiche readers, and a microfiche storage cabinet were procured for each target school. The media specialists had recommended that microfiche, rather than microfilm, be utilized. Those specialists who had practical experience with microforms overwhelmingly endorsed the use of microfiche. They claimed that searching through microfilm rolls was far more cumbersome than searching through microfiche. Selection of exactly which magazine titles would be procured in microfiche was left to the discretion of the media specialists, who were also responsible for deciding which years of a magazine would be included in the microfiche collection. Two of the specialists agreed to select a wide range of titles but to limit those titles to the recent past. One specialist chose to take only a limited number of titles but to extend the collection back a number of years.

Once the equipment and magazine collections were in place, the media specialists brought the special collection to the attention of teachers and students. Generally, this could be done during the regular library orientation sessions with classes.

Monitoring the use of the microfiche collection offered no particular change in either local staffing patterns or operating procedures. All three of the target schools had historically utilized "closed stack" periodical collections. Media center users were accustomed to completing written "call slips" in order to retrieve a needed magazine. Student library aides were, likewise, accustomed to searching the stacks on the basis of a written order. Adding tracking information to the "call slip" was a minor adaptation which allowed the media personnel to search for a needed magazine issue and also document whether or not the search had been successful. In the event the magazine was supplied, one could tell whether it had been supplied in hardcopy or fiche. If the magazine could not be supplied, the reason for the failed search could be listed on the adapted "call slip," now called a "document retrieval form." An example of the document retrieval form will be found in Appendix A.

A document retrieval form was completed for every magazine transaction. Bibiographic data on the form was supplied by the borrower; transaction tracking data was supplied by media center personnel. All document retrieval forms were collected and sent to a computer firm where the raw data was input, sorted, and tabulated. The resulting printout listed the working date, school and name of the magazine. The printout also showed how many times each title had been requested and how many of the requests had been fulfilled. The printout enumerated whether the requested title had been supplied in hardcopy or fiche. In the event of an unsuccessful search, tracking data was also tabulated into four categories:

1 In-use—the needed article was being used by another student at the time of the search.

2 Article missing—the library subscribed to the needed issue and the issue was on the shelf, but the needed article was missing.

3 Missing—the media center subscribed to the needed title, but the needed issue had been lost or stolen.

4 Unavailable—the library did not subscribe to the needed title or the appropriate issue of the title was not housed in the collection.

One computer printout was prepared for each target school. Individual printouts gave only data for a particular school. In addition, a cumulative printout was also available which listed the combined totals of the three target schools.

The research project lasted for three years. Only partial circulation statistics were available for the first two years of the project, but complete statistics were available for the third year. Several unexpected complications led to this phenomenon. The first year of the project was devoted to procuring the hardware and software. The hardware was easily obtained, but the software trickled in over a long period of time. Orders for microfiche were placed with a very large microform vendor of considerable repute. Some titles were supplied very rapidly—within a few weeks. Other orders dragged out over several months. Some delays were the result of the vendor's filming schedule; some delays were the result of the publisher's microfilming policies. In short, a considerable length of time lapsed before each of the target schools had the nucleus of a working microfiche collection.

As might be expected, the tracking of each magazine transaction also required some adjustment and fine tuning. Generally, the adaptation of the call slip to a document retrieval form was minor. The student aides quickly learned to complete the transaction form after a search had been completed. However, getting a readable computer printout required some adjustment. After a couple of meetings with the keypunch operators and computer programmers, the problems were solved and the printouts provided the kinds of information being sought. The project was well into its second year of operation, however, before accurate, standardized printouts were available. The statistics quoted later in this paper are for the third year of the project. Statistics were analyzed for the first and second years of the project and the percentages were nearly identical to those gleaned from the third-year analysis; however, since complete circulation statistics were available only for the third year of the project, the author chose to describe only that year.

Findings

The project clearly demonstrated the value of the microfiche collection. During the third year of the project, a cumulative total of 21,027 magazines were requested in the target schools. Of that total, 74 percent or 15,572 magazines were supplied in hardcopy. When hardcopy and microfiche were combined, 92 percent or 19,264 of the requested magazines were supplied. Thus, the microfiche collection led to an 18 percent rise in success rate. Less than 2 percent of the magazines requested were unavailable at the time of the search because another student was using them, and in only five instances, out of 21,027 requests, were the needed articles missing from the magazine. In only 1.6 percent of the cases were requested issues subscribed to but missing from the collection, and in only 4.7 percent of the cases was the needed magazine not available from the media center collection.

These statistics were cause for some jubilation, but they also prompted some concern. The media specialists were pleased to find that they could supply 90 percent of the requested materials. That number was in line with the American Library Association/ Association for Educational Communications and Technology guideline published in 1975.[1] The media specialists were also interested to see that without the microfiche collection they were able to supply only about 75 percent of the requested materials. This finding was of no particular surprise, as each of the media specialists had informally speculated that they were supplying about 75 percent of the requested materials. What surprised the media specialists and caused them to re-evaluate their practices was the fact that a very large number of magazine requests could be filled with a surprisingly small number of magazine titles. Mancall and Drott were reaching a similar conclusion in a bibliometric study they were conducting at about the same time the Boise project was being conducted.[2] Mancall and Drott researched which information sources students actually used in preparing research papers. The Boise project investigated which magazines students requested. The finding that most surprised the Boise media specialists was that 296 titles would have been required to fill 100 percent of the magazine requests, yet only 81 titles would be needed to supply 80 percent of the requests. Even more startling, 52 percent of all magazines requested could have been supplied through the utilization of only 20 magazine titles. A list of these 20 titles is found in Appendix B. In 1985, with an awareness of the Mancall/Drott efforts (who, in turn, cited Bradford[3]), the finding does not seem so important, but in 1981 the finding took on monumental proportions.

Even the most cursory look at the magazine circulation records reinforced "Bradford's Law." Students accessed a relatively small number of magazine titles to fill their research needs. Though media specialists in the target schools had access only to the circulation records for their respective schools, they each, independently, reached a similar conclusion. Collections which housed extended back issues of the most popular research titles would fulfill more requests than would broad collections with limited back issues. Selection patterns for the second and third years of the project reflected this philosophy.

Federal funding of the project ended with the 1980–81 school year. Since that time, the target schools have continued to fund the microfiche collection through their regular district library materials budgets. In addition, based upon the findings of the study, an additional senior high school within the district has chosen to build a microfiche collection.

Interviews

During November and December of 1984, media specialists of the original target schools were asked to comment on the value of the microfiche collections. The questions asked will be quoted exactly; however, the responses are composite summaries rather than verbatim responses.

Question 1: Can you provide any statistics to show that the success rate has remained high with microfiche?

Exact circulation statistics are not kept as they were for the federal project. However, circulation checks are carried out periodically. Those checks reveal that between 88 and 95 percent of all requests can be supplied when both hardcopy and fiche collections are accessed.

Question 2: How can we equate the extra expenditures of money in terms of higher success search rates, the quality of the products produced by students, and their attitudes toward library service?

The microfiche collection is not an "extra"; it is an integral part of our collection. The students rely on the microfiche collection. Not a single fiche has been lost, stolen, or mutilated in the history of the project. There is no worry that a heavily used issue will be lost or stolen. There is no fear that nondelivery of the hardcopy will interrupt service to students. Frustrations with jobbers and publishers remain, but the frustrations of trying to replace elusive back issues are gone. The machinery has been outstanding. The reader/printers can be temperamental, but very few of the microfiche readers have even required a bulb replacement. The students do not have to change topics anymore for lack of resources. A few magazine titles can cover many, many subjects. Throughout the history of the project we have been able to reduce the number of titles but increase the years covered in back issues. It frustrates us as media specialists that kids seem to put little value on the currency of information, but perhaps they work from such a limited knowledge and experiential base that any additional information adds to their base, even if it's old information to the adult world.

Question 3: What is the cost of student frustration?

There is no way we can answer the question. The circulation statistics clearly show that students are able to access more information with the fiche than they could without it. By using the reader/printer, the student can make a copy of the needed article and take it home or to class. Students are not so pressed to return the magazine after one day. Fifteen students can now use the same issue on the same day if the need arises. Fewer students are required to change topics now that we utilize microfiche. We can have extended back issues now. It would be very difficult to have extended back issues of *Newsweek, Time* and *U.S. News & World Report* and still not be able to find some article on some topic of some use to some student. Students no longer encounter three or four "turn-downs" in order to achieve one "hit."

Question 4: Is there any evidence that students' attitudes are better because their success rate is higher?

There is no empirical evidence, only perceptive evidence. The kids seem to be more willing to get on with the project. It's not so unusual to hear a student say "That machine gave me exactly what I wanted."

Question 5: Do you, as a media specialist, select titles based on potential of research use as well as recreational use?

Only research materials are procured in microfiche format. No one denies the importance of recreational reading. Some titles in hardcopy are selected primarily for their recreational value. The primary thrust of the project, however, has been to bolster the research collection which students must utilize in order to complete assignments.

Periodicals on Microfiche

Question 6: How well do students adapt to the use of micro-forms rather than paper copies?

Students adapt to change easily. They use personal computers, video recorders, and microwave ovens. The microfiche reader is just another tool. The students are not faced with a micro-form *or* paper decision. We still subscribe to many hardcopy magazines. The regular collection and microfiche collection have always worked in tandem. Some kids prefer the hard-copy; some kids prefer the fiche; some kids make a paper copy of the fiche article. The microformat may be obsolete right now. Within the very near future, students may have magazine articles delivered to their homes via telephone lines, satellites, and personal computers. Even now, McGraw-Hill anticipates the profitable electronic storage, sorting, and delivery of infor-mation to specialized users, including the education commu-nity.[4] In the meantime, the microfiche collection allows us to deliver 90 percent of all magazine requests.

Question 7: What policies are in effect for the storage of back issues in hardcopy?

Extended collections of back issues are the real strength of the microfiche project. School media centers have historically held to the five-year collection of back issues. There are two problems with that concept. We find it difficult to keep a pop-ular issue for five years. They are either destroyed by repeated circulations or mutilated or stolen. Once they're gone, they're practically impossible to replace—regardless of what missing copy banks claim to the contrary. What if they never arrive in the mail? What if they never survive the trip from the school's mail room to the media center? The second problem concerns the student requests. If the media center holds only a five-year collection of back issues, and if the *Readers' Guide* or other in-dexing tools are only saved for a five-year period, then why do so many students make magazine requests that extend far beyond that five-year period? We don't have to discard micro-fiche after the five-year limit. Microfiche takes so little storage space that we can hold it indefinitely. It's paid for, so why not hold onto it? Never mind the fact that we've already discarded the old *Readers' Guides*. The students still try to access old magazines. They seem to place little value on the currency of the articles they request.

The microfiche project has allowed each of us great flexibility in controlling the magazine collection. One of our media centers has very limited storage space. In that media center, microfiche copies are obtained as quickly as they are available. As soon as the fiche arrives, the hardcopies are donated to teachers who use them for classroom collections or other projects. Another of the target schools has adequate, but not ample, storage space in the media center. In this school, the hardcopies are maintained for a five-year period. Once the hardcopy has been in the collection for five years, it is replaced with a microfiche copy. The hardcopies are then donated to teachers and students. The third target school also has sufficient storage to maintain a five-year collection of hardcopies. However, in this school microfiche copies are procured as soon as they are available from the microform vendor. Thus two copies, one hardcopy and one microfiche copy, are simultaneously available for a student use. In the event magazines are donated to the media center, they are first used to replace missing issues in the hardcopy collection. Once a given title reaches the five-year limit, it is donated to teachers and students. The microfiche copies, of course, are retained.

Question 8: What storage facilities are required for microfiche and what environmental controls do they incorporate?

Microfiche is easily stored in a steel cabinet specifically designed for that purpose. The cabinet, which compares favorably to a four-drawer file cabinet, now stores the same amount of information which formerly required hundreds of linear feet of library shelving. Additional microfiche storage will not be needed for several years. Replacement of microfiche is not anticipated, either. The quality of microfiche can vary, but we suspect that the variation is more related to filming techniques and procedures and the quality of the master being filmed than it is to environmentally induced deterioration. The media specialist at one school took the precaution of storing the fiche in acid-free envelopes. Media specialists at the other two target schools stored the microfiche in the envelopes which the vendor supplied. No discernible differences are evident when the various collections are examined; however, no scientific tests have been conducted. Some of the microfiche in the collections is now seven years old. Media specialists at the target schools are unable to detect any deterioration in the quality of the microfiche, even though some of it has been heavily used. None of us feels confident enough in our scientific knowledge to venture a guess as to how well microfiche would fare in other regions. Boise enjoys a fairly moderate temperature even though the outside temperatures can vary between extremes of −20°F and +105°F. Though summer temperatures inside school buildings can be uncomfortably warm, the heat is countered by extremely low humidity. The moderate, dry climate seems to be a healthy environment for the storage of microfiche.

Conclusions and Recommendations

The microfiche project was important for several reasons, but one concept is of primary concern. The utilization of the newer technology facilitated improved media center service to students. The utilization of microfiche improved magazine service, and it also opened doors to other research activities. For example, the New York Times Company offers specialized research collections in microformats. Media specialists from the target schools have investigated some of the programs and found them to be quite useful. The programs are cost effective since they can be purchased for a reasonable price and they hold up well under heavy use.

Another valuable concept revealed through the project was the use of electronic data processing equipment to store information pertinent to collection building. Tracking each magazine transaction would have been next to impossible without using a computer. The computer work for the project was contracted through a private firm. However, modern personal computers can now reasonably handle data files which five years ago could only be handled by minicomputers and mainframes. Media specialists nationally are coming more and more to rely upon automated circulation systems which contain powerful report generators. It would seem reasonable that some of these systems could be adapted in such a way as to help specialists determine which parts of the collection are most useful for specific research purposes. These circulation patterns, in turn, could have vast implications on selection policies.

Notes

1 American Association of School Librarians, *Media Programs: District and School* (Chicago: American Library Association, 1975), p. 70.

2 Jacqueline Mancall and M. Carl Drott, *Measuring Student Information Use* (Littleton: Libraries Unlimited, 1983).

3 S. C. Bradford, *Documentation* (Washington, DC: Public Affairs, 1950).

4 "An Electronic McGraw-Hill," *Newsweek*, December 10, 1984, p. 69.

Appendix A

Document Retrieval Form

Magazine Title _____

Date of Magazine _____

Student's Name _____

For Media Center Use Only!!!

Supplied?   Yes _____   No _____

If "No," please give reason below.

In-Use _____ Article Missing _____

Magazine Missing _____   Unavailable _____

Appendix B

Twenty Most Commonly Requested Magazines— Ranked by Order of Popularity

Boise Study

1. *Newsweek*
2. *Time*
3. *U.S. News & World Report*
4. *Sports Illustrated*
5. *Business Week*
6. *Science News*
7. *Hot Rod*
8. *People*
9. *Seventeen*
10. *Consumer Reports*
11. *Scientific American*
12. *Reader's Digest*
13. *Good Housekeeping*
14. *Science Digest*
15. *Science*
16. *American Heritage*
17. *Nation*
18. *Popular Mechanics*
19. *Psychology Today*
20. *Outdoor Life*

Mancall/Drott Study

1. *Newsweek*
2. *Time*
3. *U.S. News & World Report*
4. *Sports Illustrated*
5. *New Republic*
6. *Saturday Review*
7. *Scientific American*
8. *Science Digest*
9. *Science News*
10. *Nation*
11. *Reader's Digest*
12. *Business Week*
13. *National Geographic*
14. *America*
15. *American Heritage*
16. *Science*
17. *Current History*
18. *Congressional Digest*
19. *Psychology Today*
20. *National Review*

Standard Measures for Sixteen-Millimeter Film Libraries That Support Public Schools

Marvin Davis

Over the past 30 years, sixteen-millimeter film has been one of the most widely used forms of educational media. Acceptance of this media has been so widespread that its value as a basic teaching tool goes almost unquestioned. It is, however, too expensive for a local school to have in large quantity, so centralized film libraries have been formed to spread costs over a larger clientele.

Since World War II, several types of repositories of film have been created to handle distribution to the schools. In states such as Iowa and Pennsylvania, regional centers, each with a film library, serve specified school districts within a state. In other states such as Arkansas, a state-wide film library functions to distribute titles. A third configuration is in states such as Utah and Idaho, where rental film libraries are a part of university audiovisual departments. Finally, some school districts or county boards of education (Los Angeles, for example) provide services to their respective clients.

There is very little in the professional literature that serves as a guideline or standard for a film library to meet. Size of collections, methods of distribution and many other strategies have emerged through a mutual sharing of experience, a healthy sense of competition and a dedicated effort to provide service. The following study is an effort to alleviate, to some extent, that lack of documentation.

Conditions and Size of Collection

In order for film to be effective, there must be a broad enough selection of titles available within a subject area to provide an adequate coverage of the curriculum and enough films in the collection to allow a film to be available when needed. Other factors affecting use are the effort required by the user to obtain the film, the technology available to book the film, the speed of delivery from the film library, and the speed with which a returned film is checked in and routed to a new location. In addition, the effectiveness of film is dependent on curriculum needs and teacher effectiveness as well as on the quality of production techniques, film length, and currentness of the material. Several of these factors critical to success are lodged in the local school—out of the hands of the film library staff.

While many factors are needed to make the system work, the number of titles and duplicates held by the film library is crucial. No matter what the size of the population being served by a film library, there is a need for a minimum number of titles, a critical mass, in order to cover the basic areas of the curriculum. A look at the commercial market reveals that there are approximately 20,000 sixteen-millimeter film titles available which are appropriate for elementary and secondary schools. Experience from numerous film libraries dictates that about 10 percent of the total titles available, or 2,000 different films, are needed in a film library as a "critical mass" foundation. A further breakdown by grade level shows the need for approximately 60 percent of the 2,000 titles to be targeted toward the elementary school, 15 percent toward the junior high, and 25 percent toward the high school. This breakdown allows for 60 films per subject area and grade level.

An individual teacher is not likely to use 60 film titles in a particular subject area or grade level, but most film libraries serve multiple school buildings, districts, and a variety of communities. The 60 film titles allow for variation in content, method of instruction, and timeliness of content. As the number of districts being served by the film library rises above ten, 20 percent of the total film titles available, or 4,000 titles, should be available. This enlarged base collection allows enough breadth to support the entire spectrum of elementary and secondary curricula.

The second major decision to be made by a film librarian is how many prints of a particular title should be purchased to fill the demand made by clientele. This decision is based upon several factors:

- The number of uses for each title each year
- Seasonality of topics
- Scheduling of similar topics throughout the districts

- The length of time needed by each teacher to use the film
- The number of teachers requesting the film
- The desired breadth of the collection

The number of uses per film per year may vary due to the time taken to distribute, disburse, use, and return it. Delivery by mail probably causes the most variation and is often the slowest means of transport. Other forms of commercial carrier are quicker, but the cost is usually prohibitive. Delivery which is contracted to school systems or an in-house film library delivery system provides the highest possible use per copy because there is a high degree of control over the delivery system. Film library delivery personnel can establish rapport with school personnel and thus reduce late returns and incorrect returns to a negligible amount.

One advantage of a regional film library over a school district film library is the larger variation of dates when a particular curricular topic is taught. This larger date variability will require fewer duplicate prints than would be true in a single school district.

The length of time the film is needed by a specific teacher will depend upon the availability of equipment in the school. In addition, school schedules may change for unexpected special events, such as an ice storm or a special assembly. Another factor is how well a teacher can integrate a film into a teaching schedule when the film arrives, particularly if the film had to be ordered far in advance of the anticipated showing date.

The number of users requesting a single film title can vary not only according to the size of the student population served but also according to how well the requester has received services in the past. The poorer the film service has been, the fewer the number of requests that will be made by the same service population.

A major challenge is trying to decide how many duplicates of the same film title to stock in the film library. One approach is the in-depth method, in which numerous duplicates are available but a narrower range of titles is stocked. The refusal rate or turndown rate will be low using this method, but other problems emerge. A major problem with the in-depth approach is that whole sections of the library will become dated rather rapidly and so will require a large expenditure for replacement. A second approach is to provide a wider variety of titles with fewer duplicates. This allows for more curriculum variation and a more manageable replacement schedule. The breadth approach, however, assumes that a higher turndown rate is acceptable. Many users become familiar with a specific film and hesitate to accept a substitute title even when the coverage is quite similar.

Computerized Measures

The advent of computerized record keeping has enabled film library managers to maintain a variety of records in order to have the management data needed to acquire and maintain an adequate lending operation. This management data, once collected, can be used for collection development related to requests, datedness, seasonableness, and so forth. The following recommendations are based on ten years of data collection from Iowa's 15 regional film libraries. The variation in size of service area and numbers of students and the educational philosophy of the individual school districts or intermediate unit may give an insight into what is needed to meet the instructional needs of multiple school districts served by a film library. Table 1 shows the number of films circulated per student in five Iowa film libraries.

Table 1 shows also that the student population within the 15 centers of Iowa varies from about 13,000 students to 110,000 students. The smaller centers tend to be in areas which are more sparsely populated and have smaller school districts with fewer students per classroom. The number of teachers served by a film library will vary from 800 to 6,000. An effective way to look at the film data is to compare the number of prints available per student with the turndown rate. Table 2 provides such a comparison.

The data in table 2 show the need to duplicate prints of titles at about 2,500 students if the turndown rate is to be kept low. Notice also that the average number of duplicate prints ranges from

Table 1
Circulation Per Student

Film Library	Number of Students Served	1978	1980	1982	1984
A	15,577	1.21	1.26	1.22	1.32
B	21,246	1.25	1.60	1.82	1.73
C	28,639	1.57	1.74	1.84	1.91
D	63,821	1.30	1.54	1.67	1.85
E	109,823	1.53	1.61	1.61	1.68

Standard Measures for Sixteen-Millimeter Film Libraries That Support Public Schools

Table 2
Variation of Turndowns with Student Population

Film Library	Number of Students	Print/Titles	Percentage of Turndowns
A	15,577	1.03	2
B	21,246	1.04	3
C	28,639	1.29	11
D	63,821	1.45	12
E	109,823	2.00	9

1.03 to 2. In actuality, the number of duplicates purchased per title runs from 1 to as high as 15, the latter for some subjects such as driver education which are taught primarily in the summer. The normal range for duplicates is from 1 to 8 copies per title. The amount of duplication in any film library will be a variable of the philosophy of the film library manager, i.e., an in-depth collection versus a collection of breadth.

If funding for collection development is based upon a per-pupil allocation, the number of titles purchased by each film library will be directly related to the number of students within the region. Table 3 shows this variation in the number of titles per student.

Table 3 demonstrates also that in the five Iowa regions, as the student population increases from 13,000 to 110,000, the number of titles per student increases from 1 per 5.5 students to 1 per 11.5 students. At the same time, the average number of prints per title has increased from one to two.

Table 4 compares the number of prints per title with the percentage of turndowns.

A level of 95 percent filled requests can be maintained with 1 print per title up to 25,000 students, 2 prints for 25–40,000 and

Table 3
Variation in Number of Titles per Student

Film Library	Number of Students	Number of Titles	Number of Students/ Title
A	15,577	2,858	5.5
B	21,246	3,342	6.3
C	28,639	5,520	5.1
D	63,821	6,541	9.7
E	109,823	9,500	11.5

Table 4
Variation in Turndowns with Prints/Titles

Film Library	P/T	#T	%TD	P/T	#T	%TD	P/T	#T	%TD	P/T	#T	%TD
A	1.05	2043	3	1.04	2335	3	1.03	2643	3	1.03	3888	2
B	1.13	2426	6	1.04	2670	4	1.06	2956	3	1.03	3342	3
C	1.30	3428	15	1.28	4454	13	1.25	5110	12	1.23	5520	11
D	1.64	4054	17	1.49	5440	14	1.47	6126	13	1.45	6541	12
E	1.52	6312	10	2.04	7914	10	2.02	8327	9	2.00	9500	9

P/T = Prints per title

T = Titles

TD = Percentage turndown

Standard Measures for Sixteen-Millimeter Film Libraries That Support Public Schools

3 prints for 40–60,000 students. An additional print is needed for each additional 20,000 students. This number is not applicable for seasonal use films, or narrow curriculum topics, or films that may be used for entertainment rather than to support curricula. Some of the films made from picture books are an example of material that would fall into the entertainment category if improperly used. Also, those titles that have only a limited curriculum use may only require one print per title for each 100,000 students served. An example would be in very specific areas of science, foreign language and advanced studies.

The cost of maintaining a 95 percent filled request rate may be prohibitive for many film libraries. An alternative and more realistic standard is a 90 percent filled request rate with duplicates being purchased when a film can be supplied only 85 percent of the time.

An instructive turndown rate study is provided in a case look at the Heartland Area Film Library which was destroyed by fire in 1975. Table 5 provides a summary of the usage.

During the first three years, the emphasis was on acquiring a broad selection of titles. Then, for the next three years, the emphasis was on the purchase of needed duplicate prints with limited expansion of new titles. Currently, the collection is being maintained at a level of between 17,000 and 19,000 prints.

Duplicate prints were initially purchased when there were more than 15 requests and a 20 percent turndown. In 1980 this was changed. Duplicate prints were purchased when there was a 10 percent turndown rate, and this is where it has remained. Another

Table 5
Heartland Film Library Title/Usage Rates

Year	Number of Titles	Number of Prints	Number of Uses	Percentage of Turndown
1975–76	1,513	8,323	137,470	51.3
1976–77	5,702	8,994	143,740	35.6
1977–78	6,093	9,415	153,932	25.3
1978–79	6,686	13,738	167,728	14.9
1979–80	7,914	16,150	175,432	11.5
1980–81	8,563	17,125	185,503	8.6
1981–82	9,366	17,857	181,783	9.3
1982–83	9,500	18,425	186,898	9.2
1983–84	9,500	19,000	185,069	8.9

major factor not shown in table 5 is the procedure established for delivery and pickup of films from schools. Twice-a-week van delivery and the supplying of van drivers with lists of films to be picked up at each school has allowed the library to reduce the late returns by over 20 percent. Late films constitute less than one-half of one percent. This greatly affects not only the turndown rates but the satisfaction of the users.

Other Measures

With the computerization of many film libraries, other measures of collections come into the realm of the possible. A list of these measures and their anticipated use is suggested:

Measure	Use
Number of titles per subject area	Indicates breadth of collection
Number of titles per teacher	Indicates adequacy of library
Uses per title	Indicates utilization
Turndowns per print	Indicates need for duplicate copies
Requests per print	Indicates breadth of use and need for duplicate copies
Listing of titles by copyright date	Indicates age of collection
Listing of titles by copyright date within subjects	Indicates age of collection within subjects
Total uses over lifetime of print	Shows cost/use index
Listing of title by grade level and subject area	Indicates coverage of topics
Listing of use by grade level and subject area	Indicates coverage of use
Listing of titles no longer used	Identifies dated, irrelevant material; incorrect cataloging; or inappropriate titles
Listing of high number of requests and high turndowns	Shows that duplicate or similar titles are needed
Late films by building teacher	Determines problem areas for circulation procedures and identifies problem users
Listing of unused prints	Determines where demand has changed and extra prints could be removed

Standard Measures for Sixteen-Millimeter Film Libraries That Support Public Schools

Summary

The advancement of computers has allowed film library managers to both collect and manipulate data about the collection and its users at a reasonable cost. This information has provided a basis for the replacement, expansion, and duplication of the materials, based on the users' needs.

Data would support the standard of not less than 2,000 titles as a minimum core collection needed to serve even the smallest population. One print per title will serve up to 25,000 students. An additional print is needed in major subject areas for each additional 20,000 students.

The measures identified in this article suggest a number of decision points that computerized data collection can provide. A film library manager need no longer use "guesstimates" in deciding when to duplicate titles, when to add new titles, what subject areas are in demand, what films need to be weeded from the collection and a host of other critical decisions. For the first time in the history of film libraries, a decision support system is within reach.

Contributors

Melvin McKinney Bowie is Assistant Professor in the Department of Instructional Technology at The University of Georgia, Athens. She obtained the A.B. degree in history from Tougaloo College, Tougaloo, Mississippi. She holds a M.S. degree in library science from the University of Illinois, Urbana, and the Ph.D. in curriculum and instructional media from Iowa State University, Ames. She has published articles in *School Library Media Quarterly* and *Instructional Innovator* and is the author of two books.

Marvin S. Davis is Director of Media Services at the Heartland Area Education Agency 11 in Ankeny, Iowa. Dr. Davis's media center serves the central area of Iowa, including Des Moines, and is the largest of the regional media centers in the state. He received a M.S. in education from the University of North Dakota and a Ph.D. from Iowa State University.

Barbara Dobbs is Assistant Director of Library Media Services, Aurora Public Schools, Colorado. She has been the library media specialist at East Middle School in Aurora and has a B.S. in history and library science and a M.A. in curriculum and instructional media from Eastern Michigan University.

Grace Donoho is the Library Media Specialist at the Northwest Arkansas Education Cooperative, Springdale, Arkansas. She was formerly the Library Media Specialist at the Bessie Moore Center for Economic Education, University of Arkansas, Fayetteville. She received her M.S.Ed. from the University of Arkansas.

Susan Gough is a community college librarian in Steamboat Springs, Colorado. Formerly, she was library media specialist at Laredo Elementary School in Aurora, Colorado. She has a B.S. in child development and family relationships from Colorado State University and a M.A. in elementary education from Northern Colorado University.

Contributors

Barbara Herrin is on the staff of the American Association of School Librarians in Chicago. She was formerly Associate Professor and Assistant Dean of the School of Library and Information Management, Emporia State University, Kansas. She holds a B.S. in elementary education from Phillips University, a M.L.S. from Emporia State, and a Ph.D. in educational technology from Kansas State University. She also served ten years as library media specialist for the campus laboratory school at ESU and two years as Director of Elementary Student Teaching.

May Lein Ho is Director of the Learning Resources Center at the University of Arkansas. She is from Tainan, Republic of China. She obtained a B.A. in foreign languages and literature from National Taiwan University. She holds a M.S. in educational media and technology and a M.L.S. from East Texas State University. She has a doctorate from East Texas State University in supervision, curriculum, and instruction. Dr. Ho is the author of *Appleworks for School Librarians*, published by Hi-Willow Research and Publishing Co., 1985.

David V. Loertscher is Senior Acquisitions Editor at Libraries Unlimited in Englewood, Colorado. Before that, he taught in the School of Library and Information Studies at the University of Oklahoma and in the Instructional Resources Program at the University of Arkansas. He obtained a B.S. in history from the University of Utah, a M.L.S. from the University of Washington, and a Ph.D. in library science from Indiana University. Dr. Loertscher has written for many library journals, including *School Library Media Quarterly* and *School Library Journal*. Topics of these publications have ranged from research and evaluation of school library media programs to microcomputers.

Marion Messervey (retired) was a library media specialist at Hinkley High School in Aurora, Colorado. She has an A.B. in sociology from Nebraska Wesleyan College and a M.A. in education and library science from the University of Denver.

William Murray is Director of Media Services for the Aurora Public Schools. He has an A.B. in political science from Aurora College, a M.A. in political science from Colorado College, and an administrative certificate from the University of Denver.

Contributors

Thomas H. Olsen has served as District Media Generalist for the Independent School District of Boise City since 1974. He received his B.S. from Idaho State University, his M.L.S. from the University of Washington, and his Ph.D. from Brigham Young University.

Retta Patrick (retired) was Director of Library Media Services in the Pulaski County Special School District in Little Rock, Arkansas, where she served from 1968 to 1987. She received her B.S.E. from Henderson State University and the M.L.S. from the University of Oklahoma. She has been a classroom teacher and school library media specialist at both the elementary and secondary levels and has taught graduate courses in school library media.

Louis R. Pointon holds a B.A. in French from the University of Rhode Island, a M.A.T. from Assumption College, a M.L.S. from Emporia State University, and has Ed.D. candidacy in Instructional Technology from Northern Illinois University, DeKalb. He has taught French at SUNY-Oswego and Northern Illinois, served as Director of Instructional Resources and assistant professor of education at Loras College, Dubuque, Iowa, and recently taught library science and media management at Emporia State University. He is currently studying law and law librarianship.

Sara Russell is the K-12 Library Media Specialist for Conway Springs, Kansas, Public Schools. She recently completed a B.S. in elementary education and a M.L.S. from Emporia State University, where she served as a graduate research assistant.